T5-AEZ-228

FRENCH-CANADIAN AUTHORS

A Bibliography of Their Works and of English-Language Criticism

by

MARY KANDIUK

The Scarecrow Press, Inc.
Metuchen, N.J., & London
1990

British Library Cataloguing-in-Publication data available

Library of Congress Cataloging-in-Publication Data

Kandiuk, Mary, 1956-
French-Canadian authors : a bibliography of their works and of English-language criticism / by Mary Kandiuk.
p. cm.
Includes indexes.
ISBN 0-8108-2362-4 (acid-free paper)
1. French-Canadian literature--Bibliography. 2. French-Canadian literature--History and criticism--Bibliography. I. Title.
Z1377.F8K35 1990
[PQ3901]
016.8409'9714--dc20 90-8944

Manufactured in the United States of America
Printed on acid-free paper

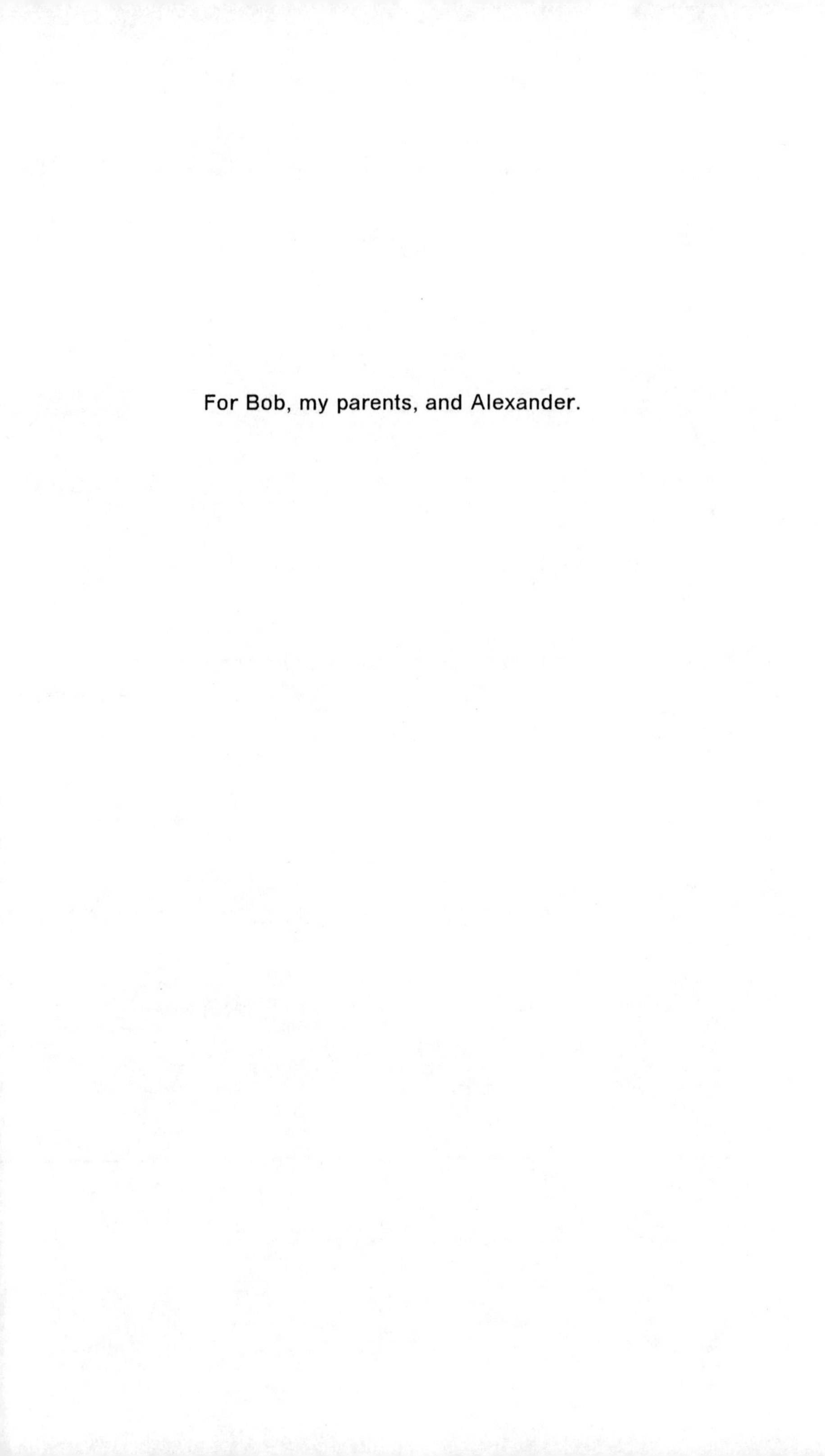

For Bob, my parents, and Alexander.

TABLE OF CONTENTS

INTRODUCTION

This work is an outgrowth of my experience as a reference librarian and Canadian literature bibliographer at York University. As interest in Canadian literature flourishes in Canada and in countries all over the world, there is an ever-increasing demand for easy access to criticism in English to assist researchers, and above all students, who are studying the works of French-Canadian authors in English translation and whose working language is English. Consultation with librarians at other universities and discussions with faculty members teaching Canadian literature confirmed this. Therefore during a recent sabbatical I set out to fill the gap in existing bibliographical tools by compiling the first bibliography of English-language criticism of French-Canadian authors.

This work was intended to include only the major French-Canadian authors for whom there existed a substantial body of criticism in English. A preliminary list of authors included those whose works were available in English translation. It is surprising how many of our French-Canadian authors are completely unavailable in English translation and how few of the works of even our more well-known and prolific French-Canadian writers have been translated. This fact limits the amount of English-language criticism that is available and hence the scope of this work. Handbooks and guides to French-Canadian literature were consulted and all of the major journals in Canadian literature and Canadian studies were searched to ensure that no authors of significant interest were overlooked. As the search for secondary sources progressed, authors were eliminated due to the lack of serious criticism in English of their works.

Secondary sources include books, parts of books, journal articles, book reviews and dissertations. Both popular and scholarly secondary materials have been included. Newspaper articles, encyclopedia articles and audio-visual materials have been excluded. Many journals and books not indexed in any of the available periodical indexes and bibliographies were searched manually, hence listings are provided for materials not available elsewhere. All entries were verified to ensure that the criticism was actually written in English and the bibliographical information correct. Criticism in English on works that have not been translated has also been included in the event that these works are translated at a later date. The cut-off date for criticism was January 1, 1989.

Each section begins with a bibliography of the author's works in chronological order. These lists are not comprehensive in that they consist of monographs only. Items such as contributions to periodicals and anthologies are not included. Reprints are also as a rule excluded. English translations of works are indicated where they exist. Following the primary bibliographies is a listing in alphabetical order by author of secondary sources in English. Brief annotations have been added to indicate the subject matter of the work when this is not obvious from the title of the entry. Annotations always use the English title of the work if it has been translated as this is the title most familiar to the English reader. If the criticism deals with four or more of the author's works then the term "overview" is used. The term "general" is used when the criticism does not focus on any particular work. A separate listing for book reviews appears at the end of the section for each author. Book reviews are arranged by work reviewed and within work alphabetically by title of the reviewing periodical. The list of book reviews is selective. Brief reviews, newspaper reviews and those reviews in obscure or minor periodicals have been omitted. Indexes to critics and editors appear at the end of the work followed by a list of addresses for Canadian publishers of journals and English-language monographs cited.

There is one person without whom this work would never have reached fruition and to whom I am deeply indebted. I would like to express sincere thanks to my husband Robert Thompson, Manager of York University Library Computing Services, who provided me with invaluable technical expertise and assistance as well as infinite moral support and encouragement. Thanks also go to the Interlibrary Loan Department of Scott Library who processed an endless number of requests for me. And last, but not least, a very special thank you to my mother, Maria Kandiuk, who greatly facilitated the completion of this work by providing countless hours of loving care to my son Alexander.

Mary Kandiuk
York University

AQUIN, HUBERT (1929-1977)

WORKS BY HUBERT AQUIN

Prochain épisode. Montreal: Cercle du Livre de France, 1965. *Prochain Episode*. Trans. Penny Williams. Toronto: McClelland and Stewart, 1967.

Trou de mémoire. Montreal: Cercle du Livre de France, 1968. *Blackout*. Trans. Alan Brown. Toronto: Anansi, 1974.

L'Antiphonaire. Montreal: Cercle du Livre de France, 1969. *The Antiphonary*. Trans. Alan Brown. Toronto: Anansi, 1973.

Point de fuite. Montreal: Cercle du Livre de France, 1971.

Neige noire. Montreal: La Presse, 1974. *Hamlet's Twin*. Trans. Sheila Fischman. Toronto: McClelland and Stewart, 1979.

Blocs erratiques: Textes (1948-1977). Ed. René Lapierre. Montreal: Quinze, 1977.

Writing Quebec: Selected Essays. Ed. Anthony Purdy. Trans. Paul Gibson. Edmonton: University of Alberta Press, 1988.

WORKS ABOUT HUBERT AQUIN

Amprimoz, Alexandre L. "Four Types of Patriotism in Quebec Letters." *Tamarack Review* 74 (1978): 60-68.
Discusses *Blocs erratiques.*

Amprimoz, Alexandre L. "Two Quebec Novels and Their Translations." *Event* 9.1 (1980): 112-17.
Discusses *Hamlet's Twin.*

Atwood, Margaret. *Survival: A Thematic Guide to Canadian Literature*. Toronto: Anansi, 1972. 227-28.
Discusses *Prochain Episode.*

Beausang, Michael. "Music and Medecine." *Canadian Literature* 58 (1973): 71-76.
Discusses *The Antiphonary.*

Bourneuf, Roland. "Literary Form and Social Reality in the Quebec Novel." *Essays on Canadian Writing* 16 (1979-1980): 219-28.
Discusses *Prochain Episode*, *Blackout* and *The Antiphonary.*

Brazeau, J. Raymond. "Hubert Aquin." *An Outline of Contemporary French Canadian Literature*. Toronto: Forum House, 1972. 75-82.
Discusses *Prochain Episode.*

Brown, Russell M. "*Blackout*: Hubert Aquin's Surreal Mystery." *Armchair Detective* 13 (1979): 58-60.

Brown, Russell M. "In Search of Lost Causes: The Canadian Novelist as Mystery Writer." *Mosaic* 11.3 (1978): 1-15.
Discusses *Blackout.*

Cagnon, Maurice. *The French Novel of Quebec*. Boston: Twayne, 1986. 98-105.
Discusses *Prochain Episode*, *Blackout* and *The Antiphonary.*

Cagnon, Maurice. "Palimpsest in the Writings of Hubert Aquin." *Modern Language Studies* 8.2 (1978): 80-89.
Discusses *Prochain Episode* and *Blackout.*

Cagnon, Maurice. "Parody and Caricature in Hubert Aquin's *L'Antiphonaire.*" *Critique* 19.2 (1977): 5-12.
Discusses *The Antiphonary.*

Cohn-Sfetcu, Ofelia. "To Live in Abundance of Life: Time in Canadian Literature." *Canadian Literature* 76 (1978): 25-36.
Discusses *Prochain Episode.*

Cohn-Sfetcu, Ofelia. "To Write or to be Written? Hubert Aquin's *Prochain Episode.*" *Modern Fiction Studies* 22.3 (1976): 449-56.

Davidson, Arnold E., and Cathy N. Davidson. "Crossing Boundaries: Hubert Aquin's *L'Antiphonaire* and Robert Kroetsch's *Gone Indian* as Fictions of the Avant-Garde." *University of Toronto Quarterly* 54.2 (1984-85): 163-77.
Discusses *The Antiphonary.*

Di Virgilio, Paul. "Literary Negativity in 'Shifting-Out': Aquin, Faulkner and Garcia Marquez." *Proceedings of the Xth Congress of the International Comparative Literature Association*: *New York 1982*. Ed. Anna Balakian. New York: Garland, 1985. 3: 107-11.
Discusses *Prochain Episode.*

Dorsinville, Max. *Caliban Without Prospero*: *Essay on Quebec and Black Literature*. Erin, Ont.: Porcépic, 1974. 105-33.
Discusses *Prochain Episode.*

Ferguson, Ted. "The Mental Inmate Who Had to Write." *Maclean's Magazine* 2 Apr. 1966: 47.
Discusses *Prochain Episode.*

Gibson, Paul. "Aquin Again." *Books in Canada* May 1982: 3.
General.

Grace, Sherrill E. "Dans le cristallin de nos yeux: *Neige Noir*, Caligari and the Postmodern Film Frame-Up." *New Comparison* 5 (1988): 89-103.
Discusses *Hamlet's Twin.*

Hajdukowski-Ahmed, Maroussia. "The Unique, Its Double and the Multiple: The Carnivalesque Hero in the Québécois Novel." Trans. Jan Marta. *Yale French Studies* 65 (1983): 139-53.
Discusses *Blackout* and *Prochain Episode.*

Harger-Grinling, V., and A. R. Chadwick. "The Play-within-the-Play: A Study of Madness in Hubert Aquin's *Neige noire.*" *The Fantastic in World Literature and the Arts*: *Selected Essays from the Fifth International Conference on the Fantastic in the Arts*. Ed. Donald E. Morse. Westport, CT: Greenwood, 1987. 123-31.
Discusses *Hamlet's Twin.*

Heidenreich, Rosmarin. "Aspects of Indeterminacy in Hubert Aquin's *Trou de mémoire.*" *Gaining Ground: European Critics on Canadian Literature.* Ed. Robert Kroetsch and Reingard M. Nischik. Western Canadian Literary Documents Series 6. Edmonton: NeWest, 1985. 40-52.
Discusses *Blackout.*

Heidenreich, Rosmarin. "Hubert Aquin's *Prochain Episode*: An Exercise in the Hermeneutics of Reading." *Revue de l'Université d'Ottawa* 57.2 (1987): 39-54.

Heidenreich, Rosmarin. "Madness as a Strategy of Communication: The Case of Hubert Aquin's *Prochain Episode.*" *Signum* 3 (numéro special) (1981): 379-91.

Hutcheon, Linda. "Formalistic Aggression and the Act of Reading." *Violence in the Canadian Novel Since 1960/dans le roman canadien depuis 1960.* Ed. Terry Goldie and Virginia Harger-Grinling. St. John's, Nfld.: Memorial University of Newfoundland, 1981. 9-23.
Discusses *Blackout.*

Hutcheon, Linda. *Narcissistic Narrative: The Metafictional Paradox.* Waterloo, Ont.: Wilfrid Laurier University Press, 1980. 155-62.
Discusses *Blackout.*

"In Memoriam." *Quill and Quire* May 1977: 27.
Biographical.

Jameson, Fredric. "Euphorias of Substitution: Hubert Aquin and the Political Novel in Quebec." *Yale French Studies* 65 (1983): 214-23.
Discusses *Prochain Episode.*

Kidd, M. E. "Theme, Metaphor and Imagination in the Works of Hubert Aquin." *Michigan Academician: Papers of the Michigan Academy of Science, Arts, and Letters* 11: 139-45.
Overview.

Krysinski, Wladimir. "Narrative Instinct and Death Instinct in the Novels of Hubert Aquin." *Semiotic Scene* 2.4 (1978): 163-65.
Overview; summary of a paper.

La Bossière, Camille R. "Hubert Aquin's Revolutionary Commedia dell'Arte of Hell: A Baroque Impasse." *Mosaic* 11.3 (1978): 119-25.
Discusses *Prochain Episode*, *Blackout* and *Hamlet's Twin.*

La Bossière, Camille R. "An Impasse: Hubert Aquin's Revolutionary Commedia dell'Arte." *The Dark Age of Enlightenment: An Essay on Quebec Literature.* Fredericton, N.B.: York Press, 1980. 31-38.
Overview.

Merivale, Patricia. "Chiaroscuro: *Neige noire/Hamlet's Twin.*" *Dalhousie Review* 60.2 (1980): 318-33.

Merivale, Patricia. "Hubert Aquin." *Canadian Writers Since 1960: First Series.* Ed. W. H. New. 1986. Dictionary of Literary Biography 53. Detroit: Gale, 1986. 8-17.
Overview.

Merivale, Patricia. "Hubert Aquin." *Profiles in Canadian Literature.* Ed. Jeffrey M. Heath. Toronto: Dundurn Press, 1982. 4: 101-08.
Overview.

Merivale, Patricia. "Hubert Aquin and Highbrow Pornography: The Aesthetics of Perversion." *Essays on Canadian Writing* 26 (1983): 1-12.
Discusses *Blackout* and *Hamlet's Twin.*

Merivale, Patricia. "Neo-Modernism in the Canadian Artist-Parable: Hubert Aquin and Brian Moore." *Canadian Review of Comparative Literature* 6.2 (1979): 195-205.
Discusses *The Antiphonary.*

Moorhead, Andrea. "Double Life: An Analysis of Hubert Aquin's *Prochain Episode.*" *Esprit Créateur* 23.3 (1983): 58-65.

"The New Montrealers: Six People Who Make Things Happen." *Maclean's Magazine* 3 Dec. 1966: 19.
General.

Purdy, Anthony. "Form and (Dis-)content: The Writer, Language, and Society in the Essays of Hubert Aquin." *French Review* 59.6 (1986): 885-93.
Discusses *Blocs erratiques* and *Point de fuite.*

"Quebec Library Honours Hubert Aquin." *Quill and Quire* May 1978: 40.
General.

Reisner, Thomas A. "De Quincey's Palimpsest Reconsidered." *Modern Language Studies* 12.2 (1982): 93-94.
General.

Ricou, Laurie. "Never Cry Wolfe: Benjamin West's *The Death of Wolfe* in *Prochain Episode* and *The Diviners*." *Essays on Canadian Writing* 20 (1980-81): 171-85.

Russell, D. W. "Hubert Aquin's *Neige Noire*: To Be or Not to Be." *Nebula* 1 (1975): 48-53.
Discusses *Hamlet's Twin.*

Russell, D. W. "To Be Or Not To Be: Creation and Destruction in Hubert Aquin's *Neige Noire.*" *Journal of Canadian Fiction* 20 (1977): 140-45.
Discusses *Hamlet's Twin.*

Shek, Ben-Zion. *Social Realism in the French-Canadian Novel*. Montreal: Harvest House, 1977. 278-81.
Discusses *Prochain Episode* and *Blackout*.

Shouldice, Larry, ed. and trans. Introduction [to "The Cultural Fatique of French Canada" by Hubert Aquin]. *Contemporary Quebec Criticism*. Ed. and trans. Larry Shouldice. Toronto: University of Toronto Press, 1979. 54-55.
Discusses critical writings.

Simon, Sherry. "Hubert Aquin: Hamlet in Quebec." *Canadian Forum* Feb. 1980: 18-21.
Overview.

Smart, Patricia. "*Neige noire*: Hamlet and Coinciding Opposites." Trans. Hélène Gallier. *Essays on Canadian Writing* 11 (1978): 97-103.
Discusses *Hamlet's Twin.*

Smart, Patricia. "Woman as Object, Women as Subjects, and the Consequences for Narrative: Hubert Aquin's *Neige Noire* and the Impasse of Post-Modernism." *Canadian Literature* 113-14 (1987): 168-78.
Discusses *Hamlet's Twin.*

Smith, Stephen. "Playing to Lose: Fictional Representations as Formulas for Failure in Aquin's *Prochain Episode.*" *Esprit Créateur* 23.3 (1983): 66-72.

Stratford, Philip. "The Uses of Ambiguity: Margaret Atwood and Hubert Aquin." *Margaret Atwood: Language, Text, and System*. Ed. Sherrill E. Grace and Lorraine Weir. Vancouver: University of British Columbia Press, 1983. 113-24. Rpt. in *All the Polarities: Comparative Studies in Contemporary Novels in French and English*. By Philip Stratford. Toronto: ECW Press, 1986. 82-95.
Discusses *Prochain Episode.*

Sugden, Leonard. "Hubert Aquin: Proteus in Despair." *Essays on Canadian Writing* 11 (1978): 73-96.
Overview.

Sutherland, Ronald. "The Fourth Separatism." *Canadian Literature* 45 (1970): 7-23.
Discusses *Prochain Episode.*

Sutherland, Ronald. Introduction. *Prochain Episode*. By Hubert Aquin. Trans. Penny Williams. New Canadian Library 84. Toronto: McClelland and Stewart, 1972. iv-viii.

Sutherland, Ronald. *Second Image: Comparative Studies in Quebec/Canadian Literature*. Toronto: New Press, 1971. 113-19.
Discusses *Prochain Episode.*

Sutherland, Ronald. "Twin Solitudes." *Canadian Literature* 31 (1967): 5-34.
Discusses *Prochain Episode.*

Urbas, Jeanette. "From Individual Revolt to Social Revolution." *From* Thirty Acres *to Modern Times: The Story of French-Canadian Literature*. Toronto: McGraw-Hill Ryerson, 1976. 138-46.
Discusses *Prochain Episode.*

Whitfield, Agnes. "Reading the Post-1960 Quebec Novel." *Esprit Créateur* 23.3 (1983): 32-39.
Discusses *Prochain Episode.*

BOOK REVIEWS

THE ANTIPHONARY/L'ANTIPHONAIRE

Books in Canada July-Sept. 1973: 4.
Canadian Fiction Magazine 17 (1975): 115-17.
Canadian Forum Nov.-Dec. 1973: 33-34.
Quarry 22.4 (1973): 74-75.
Queen's Quarterly 81.2 (1974): 313-14.
Quill and Quire June 1973: 13.
Saturday Night Sept. 1973: 41.
University of Toronto Quarterly 43.4 (1974): 343.

BLACKOUT/TROU DE MEMOIRE

Books in Canada Mar. 1975: 12-13.
Brick 2 (1978): 56.
Canadian Literature 67 (1976): 109-12.
Quill and Quire Mar. 1975: 20.
University of Toronto Quarterly 44.4 (1975): 311.

HAMLET'S TWIN/NEIGE NOIRE

Books in Canada Aug.-Sept. 1979: 11-12.
Canadian Forum Sept. 1979: 28-29.
Canadian Literature 88 (1981): 104-05.
Fiddlehead 126 (1980): 163-66.
French Review 51.1 (1977): 130-31.
Journal of Canadian Studies 14.3 (1979): 142-44.
Maclean's 21 May 1979: 57-58.
Queen's Quarterly 87.1 (1980): 161-63.
Quill and Quire Apr. 1979: 29.
University of Toronto Quarterly 49.4 (1980): 385-86.

POINT DE FUITE

Times Literary Supplement 19 May 1972: 583.

PROCHAIN EPISODE

Canadian Literature 29 (1966): 64-66.
Journal of Canadian Fiction 1.2 (1972): 92-96.
Tamarack Review 46 (1968): 109-13.
University of Toronto Quarterly 37.4 (1968): 384-85.

BEAUCHEMIN, YVES (1941-)

WORKS BY YVES BEAUCHEMIN

L'Enfirouapé. Montreal: La Presse, 1974.

Le Matou. Montreal: Québec/Amérique, 1981. *The Alley Cat*. Trans. Sheila Fischman. Toronto: McClelland and Stewart, 1986.

Cybèle. Montreal: Art Global, 1982.

Du sommet d'un arbre. Montreal: Québec/Amérique, 1986.

WORKS ABOUT YVES BEAUCHEMIN

Cagnon, Maurice. *The French Novel of Quebec*. Boston: Twayne, 1986. 136-41.
Discusses *The Alley Cat*.

Henighan, Stephen. "Myths of Making It: Structure and Vision in Richler and Beauchemin." *Essays on Canadian Writing* 36 (1988): 22-37.
Discusses *The Alley Cat*.

Manguel, Alberto. "Yves Beauchemin." *Canadian Writers Since 1960: Second Series*. Ed. W. H. New. Dictionary of Literary Biography 60. Detroit: Gale, 1987. 3-5.
Overview.

Mitchell, Constantina, and Paul Raymond Coté. "Beauchemin's *The Alley Cat* as Modern Myth." *American Review of Canadian Studies* 17.4 (1987-88): 409-18.

Parris, David L. "Cats in the Literature of Quebec." *British Journal of Canadian Studies* 3.2 (1988): 259-66.
Discusses *The Alley Cat*.

Turbide, Diane. "Two Solitudes: The Publishing History of Yves Beauchemin's Acclaimed Novel *Le matou*, Shows the Gap Between Canada's English and French Literary Worlds." *Saturday Night* Dec. 1984: 59-60.
Discusses *The Alley Cat*.

BOOK REVIEWS

THE ALLEY CAT/LE MATOU

Books in Canada Aug.-Sept. 1986: 17-18.
Canadian Book Review Annual (1987): 114.
Canadian Literature 113-14 (1987): 249-51.
Cross-Canada Writers' Quarterly 8.3-4 (1986): 36-37.
French Review 55.6 (1982): 920-21.
Maclean's 28 Apr. 1986: 57-58.
Malahat Review 77 (1986): 132-34.
New York Times Book Review 11 Jan. 1987: 14.
Queen's Quarterly 94.1 (1987): 252.
Quill and Quire Apr. 1986: 36.
University of Toronto Quarterly 57.1 (1987): 97-98.

BEAULIEU, VICTOR-LEVY (1945-)

WORKS BY VICTOR-LEVY BEAULIEU

Mémoires d'outre-tonneau. Montreal: Editions Estérel, 1968.

La Nuitte de Malcolmm Hudd. Montreal: Editions du Jour, 1969.

Race de monde! Montreal: Editions du Jour, 1969.

Jos Connaissant. Montreal: Editions du Jour, 1970; rev. Montreal: VLB, 1978. *Jos Connaissant*. Trans. Ray Chamberlain. Toronto: Exile, 1982.

Les Grands-pères. Montreal: Editions du Jour, 1971; rev. Montreal: VLB, 1979. *The Grandfathers*. Trans. Marc Plourde. Montreal: Harvest House, 1974.

Pour saluer Victor Hugo. Montreal: Editions du Jour, 1971.

Jack Kérouac: essai-poulet. Montreal: Editions du Jour, 1972. *Jack Kerouac: A Chicken-Essay*. Trans. Sheila Fischman. Toronto: Coach House Press, 1975.

Un Rêve québécois. Montreal: Editions du Jour, 1972; rev. Montreal: VLB, 1977. *A Québécois Dream*. Trans. Ray Chamberlain. Toronto: Exile, 1978.

Oh Miami, Miami, Miami. Montreal: Editions du Jour, 1973.

Don Quichotte de la démanche. Montreal: L'Aurore, 1974. *Don Quixote in Nighttown*. Trans. Sheila Fischman. Erin, Ont.: Porcépic, 1978.

En attendant Trudot. Montreal: L'Aurore, 1974.

Manuel de la petite littérature du Québec. Montreal: L'Aurore, 1974.

Blanche forcée. Montreal: L'Aurore, 1975; rev. Montreal: VLB, 1976.

Ma corriveau: suivi de La Sorcellerie en finale sexuée. Montreal: VLB, 1976.

N'évoque plus que le désenchantement de ta ténèbre, mon si pauvre Abel: lamentation. Montreal: VLB, 1976.

Monsieur Zéro. Montreal: VLB, 1977.

Sagamo Job J. Montreal: VLB, 1977.

Cérémonial pour l'assassinat d'un ministre. Montreal: VLB, 1978.

Monsieur Melville. 3 vols. Montreal: VLB, 1978. *Monsieur Melville*. 3 vols. Trans. Ray Chamberlain. Toronto: Coach House Press, 1984.

La Tête de Monsieur Ferron ou les Chians. Montreal: VLB, 1979.

Una. Montreal: VLB, 1980.

Satan Belhumeur. Montreal: VLB, 1981. *Satan Belhumeur*. Trans. Ray Chamberlain. Toronto: Exile, 1983.

Moi, Pierre Leroy, prophète, martyr et un peu fêlé du chaudron: plagiaire. Montreal: VLB, 1982.

Discours de Samm. Montreal: VLB, 1983.

Entre la sainteté et le terrorisme. Montreal: VLB, 1984.

Steven Le Hérault. Montreal: Stanké, 1985. *Steven Le Hérault*. Trans. Ray Chamberlain. Toronto: Exile, 1987.

Chroniques polissonnes d'un téléphage enragé. Montreal: Stanké, 1986.

L'Héritage. Montreal: Entreprises Radio-Canada, 1987.

WORKS ABOUT VICTOR-LEVY BEAULIEU

Cagnon, Maurice. *The French Novel of Quebec*. Boston: Twayne, 1986. 122-26.
Discusses *La Nuitte de Malcolmm Hudd*, *A Québécois Dream* and *Monsieur Melville*.

Chamberlain, Ray. "Beaulieu his dream." *Brick* 9 (1980): 33-35.
Discusses *À Québécois Dream.*

Chamberlain, Raymond. "VLB: Writer, Publisher, Mystic." *Canadian Forum* Feb. 1980: 15-17.
Interview.

Ellenwood, Ray. "Avee-voo Loo Victor-Levy Bowlyoo?" *Brick* 9 (1980): 36-46.
Overview.

Gauvin, Lise. "From Octave Crémazie to Victor-Lévy Beaulieu: Language, Literature and Ideology." Trans. Emma Henderson. *Yale French Studies* 65 (1983): 30-49.
General.

Kröller, Eva-Marie. "Postmodernism, Colony, Nation: The Melvillean Texts of Bowering and Beaulieu." *Revue de l'Université d'Ottawa* 54.2 (1984): 53-61.
Discusses *Monsieur Melville.*

Kröller, Eva-Marie. "Victor-Lévy Beaulieu." *Canadian Writers Since 1960: First Series*. Ed. W. H. New. Dictionary of Literary Biography 53. Detroit: Gale, 1986. 42-48.
Overview.

May, Cedric. "Canadian Writing: Beautiful Losers in Presqu'Amérique." *Bulletin of Canadian Studies* 3.2 (1979): 5-18.
Discusses *La Nuitte de Malcolmm Hudd.*

Reid, Malcolm. "Writing After the Quiet Revolution." *Quill and Quire* May 1976: 8-9.
Overview.

BOOK REVIEWS

BLANCHE FORCEE

World Literature Today 53.3 (1979): 471.

DON QUIXOTE IN NIGHTTOWN/DON QUICHOTTE DE LA DEMANCHE

Books in Canada June-July (1978): 17.
Canadian Fiction Magazine 30-31 (1979): 225-26.
Canadian Forum June-July (1978): 39-40.
Canadian Literature 88 (1981): 100-04.
Quill and Quire June 1978: 43.
Times Literary Supplement 14 May 1976: 578.
University of Toronto Quarterly 48.4 (1979): 386-88.

EN ATTENDANT TRUDOT

Canadian Literature 63 (1975): 115-16.

THE GRANDFATHERS/LES GRANDS-PERES

Books in Canada Oct. 1975: 21.
Canadian Book Review Annual (1975): 98.
Canadian Literature 88 (1981): 93-96.
Chelsea Journal Mar.-Apr. 1976: 83-85.
Fiddlehead 108 (1976): 106-07.
Journal of Canadian Fiction 19 (1977): 130-33.
Queen's Quarterly 83.2 (1976): 349-51.
Quill and Quire Oct. 1975: 17.
University of Toronto Quarterly 45.4 (1976): 323.

JACK KEROUAC: A CHICKEN-ESSAY/JACK KEROUAC: ESSAI-POULET

Canadian Book Review Annual (1976): 220.
Canadian Literature 80 (1979): 71-72.
Journal of Canadian Fiction 19 (1977): 130-33.
Modern Fiction Studies 23.4 (1977-78): 664.
Quill and Quire 15 Apr. 1976: 6.
Times Literary Supplement 14 May 1976: 578.

JOS CONNAISSANT

Books in Canada Mar. 1983: 25-26.
Canadian Book Review Annual (1982): 137.
University of Toronto Quarterly 52.4 (1983): 395-96.

MANUEL DE LA PETITE LITTERATURE DU QUEBEC

Times Literary Supplement 14 May 1976: 578.

MONSIEUR MELVILLE

British Journal of Canadian Studies 1.1 (1986): 171.
Canadian Forum Feb. 1980: 35-36.
Canadian Literature 110 (1986): 137-39.
Maclean's 2 Apr. 1979: 42+.
University of Toronto Quarterly 56.1 (1986): 76-77.

OH MIAMI, MIAMI, MIAMI

Journal of Canadian Fiction 3.2 (1974): 102-03.

A QUEBECOIS DREAM/UN REVE QUEBECOIS

Brick 9 (1980): 31-33.
Canadian Forum Feb. 1980: 34.
Journal of Canadian Fiction 2.1 (1973): 87.
Quill and Quire Dec. 1979: 25.
University of Toronto Quarterly 50.4 (1981): 78-79.

RACE DE MONDE!

Canadian Literature 88 (1981): 127-33.

SATAN BELHUMEUR

Quill and Quire Mar. 1982: 64.

STEVEN LE HERAULT

Books in Canada June-July 1987: 20.
Canadian Book Review Annual (1987): 115.
Quill and Quire Apr. 1987: 28.
University of Toronto Quarterly 58.1 (1988): 90-92.

LA TETE DE MONSIEUR FERRON OU LES CHIANS

Canadian Theatre Review 30 (1981): 124-25.

UNA

Canadian Literature 91 (1981): 126-27.

BERSIANIK, LOUKY (1930-)

(Pseud. of Lucile Durand)

WORKS BY LOUKY BERSIANIK

Koumic, le petit Esquimau. Montreal: Centre de Psychologie et de Pédagogie, 1964.

Le Cordonnier Pamphille, Mille-pattes. Montreal: Centre de Psychologie et de Pédagogie, 1965.

La Montagne et l'escargot. Montreal: Centre de Psychologie et de Pédagogie, 1965.

Togo, apprenti-remorqueur. Montreal: Centre de Psychologie et de Pédagogie, 1965.

L'Euguélionne. Montreal: La Presse, 1976. *The Euguélionne*. Trans. Gerry Denis, Alison Hewitt, Donna Murray and Martha O'Brien. Victoria: Porcépic, 1981.

La Page de garde. St-Jacques-le-Mineur, Que.: Editions de la Maison, 1978.

Le Pique-nique sur l'Acropole. Montreal: VLB, 1979.

Maternative: les pré-Ancyl. Montreal: VLB, 1980.

Les Agénésies du vieux monde. Outremont, Que.: L'Intégrale, 1982. "Agenesias of the Old World." Trans. Miranda Hay and Lise Weil. *Trivia* 7 (Summer 1985): 33-47.

Au beau milieu de moi. Montreal: Nouvelle Optique, 1983.

Axes et eau. Montreal: VLB, 1984.

Kerameikos. Saint-Lambert, Que.: Editions du Noroit, 1987.

WORKS ABOUT LOUKY BERSIANIK

Arbour, Kathryn Mary. *French Feminist Revisions: Wittig, Rochefort, Bersianik and D'Eaubonne Rewrite Utopia*. Diss. University of Michigan, 1984.
Discusses *The Eugélionne* and *Le Pique-nique sur l'Acropole.*

Cagnon, Maurice. *The French Novel of Quebec*. Boston: Twayne, 1986. 130-33.
Discusses *The Eugélionne* and *Le Pique-nique sur l'Acropole.*

"Feminist Author Becomes Lyricist." *Canadian Composer* Mar. 1983: 24-27.
Biographical.

Gould, Karen. "Female Tracings: Writing as Re-Vision in the Recent Works of Louky Bersianik, Madeleine Gagnon, and Nicole Brossard." *American Review of Canadian Studies* 13.2 (1983): 74-89.
Overview.

Gould, Karen. "Quebec Feminists Look Back: Inventing the Text Through History." *Québec Studies* 1.1 (1983): 298-308.
Discusses *Le Pique-nique sur l'Acropole.*

Gould, Karen. "Setting Words Free: Feminist Writing in Quebec." *Signs* 6.4 (1981): 617-42.
Discusses *The Eugélionne* and *Le Pique-nique sur l'Acropole.*

Gould, Karen. "Spatial Poetics, Spatial Politics: Quebec Feminists on the City and Countryside." *American Review of Canadian Studies* 12.1 (1982): 1-9.
Discusses *Maternative.*

Hajdukowski-Ahmed, Maroussia. "Louky Bersianik: Feminist Dialogisms." *Traditionalism, Nationalism, and Feminism: Women Writers of Quebec*. Ed. Paula Gilbert Lewis. Westport, CT: Greenwood, 1985. 205-25.
Discusses *The Eugélionne, Maternative* and *Le Pique-nique sur l'Acropole.*

Neuman, Shirley. "Importing Difference." *A Mazing Space: Writing Canadian Women Writing*. Ed. Shirley Neuman and Smaro Kamboureli. Edmonton: Longspoon, 1986. 392-405.
Discusses *The Euguélionne* and *Le Pique-nique sur l'Acropole.*

Smart, Patricia. "Louky Bersianik." *Canadian Writers Since 1960: Second Series*. Ed. W. H. New. Dictionary of Literary Biography 60. Detroit: Gale, 1987. 11-16.
Overview.

Waelti-Walters, Jennifer. "And Dwelt Among Us (Bersianik)." *Fairy Tales and the Female Imagination*. Montreal: Eden, 1982. 113-33.
Discusses *The Euguélionne.*

Waelti-Walters, Jennifer. "The Food of Love: Plato's Banquet and Bersianik's Picnic." *Atlantis* 6.1 (1980): 97-103.
Discusses *Le Pique-nique sur l'Acropole.*

Waelti-Walters, Jennifer. Introduction. *The Euguélionne*. By Louky Bersianik. Trans. Gerry Denis, Alison Hewitt, Donna Murray and Martha O'Brien. Victoria: Porcépic, 1981. 5-8.

Waelti-Walters, Jennifer. "When caryatids move: Bersianik's view of culture." *A Mazing Space: Writing Canadian Women Writing*. Ed. Shirley Neuman and Smaro Kamboureli. Edmonton: Longspoon, 1986. 298-306.
Discusses *The Euguélionne, Le Pique-nique sur l'Acropole* and *Maternative.*

BOOK REVIEWS

THE EUGUELIONNE/L'EUGUELIONNE

Atlantis 2.1 (1976): 127-29.
Books in Canada Feb. 1982: 11+.
Broadside Apr. 1982: 16.
Canadian Book Review Annual (1982): 138.
Canadian Literature 102 (1984): 130-33.
Canadian Women's Studies/Les cahiers de la femme 4.2 (1982): 93-94.
University of Toronto Quarterly 51.4 (1982): 402-03.

MATERNATIVE

French Review 55.4 (1982): 563-64.

LE PIQUE-NIQUE SUR L'ACROPOLE

Canadian Literature 88 (1981): 127-33.
French Review 54.4 (1981): 615-16.

BESSETTE, GERARD (1920-)

WORKS BY GERARD BESSETTE

Poèmes temporels. Monte Carlo: Editions Regain, 1954.

La Bagarre. Montreal: Cercle du Livre de France, 1958. *The Brawl*. Trans. Marc Lebel and Ronald Sutherland. Montreal: Harvest House, 1976.

Les Images en poésie canadienne-française. Montreal: Beauchemin, 1960.

Le Libraire. Paris: Julliard, 1960. *Not for Every Eye*. Trans. Glen Shortliffe. Toronto: Macmillan, 1962.

Les Pédagogues. Montreal: Cercle du Livre de France, 1961.

L'Incubation. Montreal: Déom, 1965. *Incubation*. Trans. Glen Shortliffe. Toronto: Macmillan, 1967.

Histoire de la littérature canadienne-française par les textes: des origines à nos jours. With Lucien Geslin and Charles Parent. Montreal: Centre Educatif et Culturel, 1968.

Une Littérature en ébullition. Montreal: Editions du Jour, 1968.

Le Cycle. Montreal: Editions du Jour, 1971. *The Cycle*. Trans. A. D. Martin-Sperry. Toronto: Exile, 1987.

Trois romanciers québécois. Montreal: Editions du Jour, 1973.

La Commensale. Montreal: Quinze, 1975.

Les Anthropoïdes. Montreal: La Presse, 1977.

Mes romans et moi. Montreal: Editions Hurtubise HMH, 1979.

Le Semestre. Montreal: Québec/Amérique, 1979.

La Garden-Party de Christophine. Montreal: Québec/Amérique, 1980.

Les Dires d'Omer Marin. Montreal: Québec/Amérique, 1985.

WORKS ABOUT GERARD BESSETTE

Amprimoz, Alexandre L. "Four Writers and Today's Quebec." *Tamarack Review* 70 (1977): 72-80.
Discusses *La Commensale.*

Brazeau, J. Raymond. "Gérard Bessette." *An Outline of Contemporary French Canadian Literature.* Toronto: Forum House, 1972. 29-48.
Overview.

Cagnon, Maurice. *The French Novel of Quebec.* Boston: Twayne, 1986. 67-74.
Overview.

Dorsinville, Max. *Caliban Without Prospero: Essay on Quebec and Black Literature.* Erin, Ont.: Porcépic, 1974. 105-33.
Discusses *Not for Every Eye.*

Edwards, Mary Jane. "Gérard Bessette: A Tribute." *Canadian Literature* 88 (1981): 6-18.
Interview.

Leduc-Park, Renée. "Gérard Bessette." *Profiles in Canadian Literature.* Ed. Jeffrey M. Heath. Toronto: Dundurn Press, 1986. 6: 25-31.
Overview.

May, Cedric. *Breaking the Silence: The Literature of Québec.* Birmingham, Eng.: University of Birmingham, Regional Studies Centre, 1981. 97-99.
Discusses *Not for Every Eye.*

Perron, Paul. "On Language and Writing in Gérard Bessette's Fiction." Trans. Brian Massumi. *Yale French Studies* 65 (1983): 227-45.
Discusses *Incubation* and *Not for Every Eye.*

Raoul, Valerie. "Documents of Non-Identity: The Diary Novel in Quebec." *Yale French Studies* 65 (1983): 187-200.
Discusses *Not for Every Eye.*

Seliwoniuk, Jadwiga. "Gérard Bessette and His Dream of 'Genarration.'" *Yale French Studies* 65 (1983): 247-55.
Discusses *Le Semestre.*

Shek, Ben-Z. "Gérard Bessette and Social Realism." *Canadian Modern Language Review* 31.4 (1975): 292-300.
Overview.

Shek, Ben-Zion. "Gérard Bessette." *Canadian Writers Since 1960: First Series*. Ed. W. H. New. Dictionary of Literary Biography 53. Detroit: Gale, 1986. 49-60.
Overview.

Shek, Ben-Zion. *Social Realism in the French Canadian Novel.* Montreal: Harvest House, 1977. 230-35, 282-87.
Overview.

Shortliffe, Glen. "The Disease of Translation." *Meta* 14.1 (1969): 22-26.
Discusses *Incubation.*

Shortliffe, Glen. "Evolution of a Novelist: Gérard Bessette." *Queen's Quarterly* 74.1 (1967): 36-60.
Overview.

Shouldice, Larry, ed. and trans. Introduction [to "Psychoanalytic Criticism" by Gérard Bessette]. *Contemporary Quebec Criticism*. Ed. and trans. Larry Shouldice. Toronto: University of Toronto Press, 1979. 161-62.
Discusses critical writings.

Smith, Donald. "Gérard Bessette: Social Irony and Subconscious Impulse." *Voices of Deliverance: Interviews with Quebec and Acadian Writers*. Trans. Larry Shouldice. Toronto: Anansi, 1986. 105-26.
Interview.

Sugden, Leonard W. "Gérard Bessette's *L'incubation.*" *Journal of Canadian Fiction* 3.2 (1974): 82-84.
Discusses *Incubation.*

Sugden, Leonard W. "The Unending Cycle." *Canadian Literature* 63 (1975): 64-72.
Discusses *The Cycle.*

Sutherland, Ronald. "Brawling with Gérard Bessette." *Ariel* 4.3 (1973): 29-37.
Discusses *The Brawl.*

Sutherland, Ronald. *The New Hero: Essays in Comparative Quebec/Canadian Literature*. Toronto: Macmillan, 1977. 56-63.
Discusses *The Brawl.*

Sutherland, Ronald. *Second Image: Comparative Studies in Quebec/Canadian Literature*. Toronto: New Press, 1971. 13-15.
Discusses *The Brawl.*

Sutherland, Ronald. "Twin Solitudes." *Canadian Literature* 31 (1967): 5-24.
Discusses *The Brawl.*

Tougas, Gérard. *History of French-Canadian Literature*. Trans. Alta Lind Cook. 2nd ed. Toronto: Ryerson Press, 1966. 187-90, 229-30.
Discusses *The Brawl*, *Not for Every Eye* and *Les Pédagogues.*

Urbas, Jeanette. *From* Thirty Acres *to Modern Times: The Story of French-Canadian Literature*. Toronto: McGraw-Hill Ryerson, 1976. 85-92, 130-33.
Discusses *Not for Every Eye* and *Incubation.*

BOOK REVIEWS

LES ANTHROPOIDES

Canadian Fiction Magazine 32-33 (1979-80): 167-71.
Journal of Canadian Fiction 24 (1979): 127-30.
Quill and Quire May 1978: 45.

THE BRAWL/LA BAGARRE

Canadian Book Review Annual (1976): 147.
Canadian Forum Nov. 1977: 39-40.
Queen's Quarterly 68.1 (1961): 180-81.

LA COMMENSALE

Canadian Fiction Magazine 32-33 (1979-80): 167-71.

THE CYCLE/LE CYCLE

Books in Canada Apr. 1988: 34.
Canadian Book Review Annual (1987): 115.
Canadian Literature 91 (1981): 117-20.
University of Toronto Quarterly 58.1 (1988): 87-88.

LA GARDEN-PARTY DE CHRISTOPHINE

Canadian Literature 91 (1981): 117-20.

LES IMAGES EN POESIE CANADIENNE-FRANÇAISE

Canadian Literature 7 (1961): 80-81.

INCUBATION/L'INCUBATION

Canadian Literature 36 (1968): 62-67.
Queen's Quarterly 74.4 (1967): 768.
Tamarack Review 46 (1968): 109-13.
University of Toronto Quarterly 37.4 (1968): 385.

MES ROMANS ET MOI

Canadian Fiction Magazine 32-33 (1979-80): 167-71.

NOT FOR EVERY EYE/LE LIBRAIRE

Canadian Book Review Annual (1977): 108.
Canadian Book Review Annual (1984): 176.
Canadian Forum May 1962: 48.
Canadian Literature 12 (1962): 65-67.
Culture 23 (1962): 320.
Queen's Quarterly 68.1 (1961): 180-81.
Queen's Quarterly 69.2 (1962): 302-04.
University of Toronto Quarterly 32.4 (1963): 404.

POEMES TEMPORELS

University of Toronto Quarterly 25.2 (1956): 381-82.

LE SEMESTRE

French Review 54.3 (1981): 499-500.
World Literature Today 54.4 (1980): 594-95.

BLAIS, MARIE-CLAIRE (1939-)

WORKS BY MARIE-CLAIRE BLAIS

La Belle Bête. Quebec: Institut littéraire du Québec, 1959. *Mad Shadows*. Trans. Merloyd Lawrence. Toronto: McClelland and Stewart, 1960.

Tête blanche. Quebec: Institut littéraire du Québec, 1960. *Tête Blanche*. Trans. Charles Fullman. Toronto: McClelland and Stewart, 1961.

Le Jour est noir. Montreal: Editions du Jour, 1962. *The Day is Dark, and Three Travelers*. Trans. Derek Coltman. New York: Farrar, Straus and Giroux, 1967.

Pays voilés. Quebec: Garneau, 1963. *Veiled Countries*; *Lives*. Trans. Michael Harris. Montreal: Vehicule, 1984.

Existences. Quebec: Garneau, 1964. *Veiled Countries*; *Lives*. Trans. Michael Harris. Montreal: Vehicule, 1984.

Une Saison dans la vie d'Emmanuel. Montreal: Editions du Jour, 1965. *A Season in the Life of Emmanuel*. Trans. Derek Coltman. New York: Farrar, Straus and Giroux, 1966.

L'Insoumise. Montreal: Editions du Jour, 1966. *The Fugitive*. Trans. David Lobdell. Ottawa: Oberon, 1978.

David Sterne. Montreal: Editions du Jour, 1967. *David Sterne*. Trans. David Lobdell. Toronto: McClelland and Stewart, 1973.

L'Exécution. Montreal: Editions du Jour, 1968. *The Execution*. Trans. David Lobdell. Vancouver: Talonbooks, 1976.

Manuscrits de Pauline Archange. Montreal: Editions du Jour, 1968. *The Manuscripts of Pauline Archange*. Trans. Derek Coltman. New York: Farrar, Straus and Giroux, 1969.

Vivre! Vivre! Montreal: Editions du Jour, 1969. *The Manuscripts of Pauline Archange.* Part Two. Trans. Derek Coltman. New York: Farrar, Straus and Giroux, 1970.

Les Voyageurs sacrés. Montreal: HMH, 1969. *The Day is Dark, and Three Travelers.* Trans. Derek Coltman. New York: Farrar, Straus and Giroux, 1967.

Les Apparences. Montreal: Editions du Jour, 1970. *Dürer's Angel.* Trans. David Lobdell. Vancouver: Talonbooks, 1976.

Le Loup. Montreal: Editions du Jour, 1972. *The Wolf.* Trans. Sheila Fischman. Toronto: McClelland and Stewart, 1974.

Un Joualonais, sa joualonie. Montreal: Editions du Jour, 1973. *St. Lawrence Blues.* Trans. Ralph Manheim. New York: Farrar, Straus and Giroux, 1974.

Fièvre, et autres textes dramatiques. Montreal: Editions du Jour, 1974.

Une Liaison parisienne. Montreal: Quinze, 1975. *A Literary Affair.* Trans. Sheila Fischman. Toronto: McClelland and Stewart, 1979.

La Nef des sorcières. With Nicole Brossard, Marthe Blackburn, Luce Guilbeault, France Théoret, Odette Gagnon and Pol Pelletier. Montreal: Quinze, 1976. *A Clash of Symbols.* Trans. Linda Gaboriau. Toronto: Coach House Press Manuscript Editions, 1979.

L'Océan, suivi de Murmures. Montreal: Quinze, 1977. *The Ocean.* Trans. Ray Chamberland. Toronto: Exile, 1977. "Murmurs." Trans. Margaret Rose. *Canadian Drama/L'art dramatique canadien* 5.2 (1979): 281-93.

Les Nuits de l'underground. Montreal: Stanké, 1978. *Nights in the Underground.* Trans. Ray Ellenwood. Don Mills, Ont.: Musson, 1979.

Le Sourd dans la ville. Montreal: Stanké, 1979. *Deaf to the City.* Trans. Carol Dunlop. Toronto: Lester, Orpen and Dennys, 1981.

Visions d'Anna, ou le vertige. Montreal: Stanké, 1982. *Anna's World.* Toronto: Lester, Orpen and Dennys, 1985.

Pierre, la guerre du printemps 81. Montreal: Primeur, 1984.

Sommeil d'hiver. Montreal: Editions de la pleine lune, 1984.

L'île. Montreal: VLB, 1988.

WORKS ABOUT MARIE-CLAIRE BLAIS

Amprimoz, Alexandre L. "Four Writers and Today's Quebec." *Tamarack Review* 70 (1977): 72-80.
Discusses *A Literary Affair*.

Amprimoz, Alexandre L. "Reflections on the Novels of Marie-Claire Blais." *Event* 10.1 (1981): 134-37.
Overview.

Andersen, Margret. "The Church in Marie-Claire Blais's *A Season in the Life of Emmanuel*." *Sphinx* 2.3 (1977): 40-46.

Atwood, Margaret. Introduction. *St. Lawrence Blues*. By Marie-Claire Blais. Trans. Ralph Manheim. New York: Bantam, 1976. vii-xvi.

Atwood, Margaret. "Marie-Claire Blais is Not for Burning." *Maclean's* Sept. 1975: 26-29.
General.

Atwood, Margaret. *Survival: A Thematic Guide to Canadian Literature*. Toronto: Anansi, 1972. 223-27.
Discusses *A Season in the Life of Emmanuel*.

Brazeau, J. Raymond. "Marie-Claire Blais." *An Outline of Contemporary French Canadian Literature*. Toronto: Forum House, 1972. 99-117.
Overview.

Cagnon, Maurice. *The French Novel of Quebec*. Boston: Twayne, 1986. 106-12.
Overview.

Callaghan, Barry. "An Interview with Marie-Claire Blais." *Tamarack Review* 37 (1965): 29-34.

Coldwell, Joan. "*Mad Shadows* As Psychological Fiction." *Journal of Canadian Fiction* 2.4 (1973): 65-67.

Cotnoir, Louise. "Woman/Women on stage." *A Mazing Space: Writing Canadian Women Writing*. Ed. Shirley Neuman and Smaro Kamboureli. Edmonton: Longspoon, 1986. 307-11.
Discusses *La Nef des sorcières.*

Davis, Marilyn I. "*La Belle Bête*: Pilgrim Unto Life." *Tamarack Review* 16 (1960): 51-59.
Discusses *Mad Shadows.*

Dawson, Anthony B. "Coming of Age in Canada." *Mosaic* 11.3 (1978): 47-62.
Discusses *The Manuscripts of Pauline Archange.*

Ellenwood, Ray. "Some Notes on the Politics of Translation." *Atkinson Review of Canadian Studies* 2.1 (1984): 25-28.
Discusses *St. Lawrence Blues.*

Fitzpatrick, Marjorie A. "Teaching French-Canadian Civilization Through the Literature: Hémon, Roy, and Blais." *Québec Studies* 2 (1984): 82-93.
Discusses *A Season in the Life of Emmanuel.*

Forsyth, Louise H. "Some Reflections on the Novels of Marie-Claire Blais." *Resources for Feminist Research/Documentation sur la recherche feministe* 12.1 (1983): 16-18.
Overview.

Fouchereaux, Jean. "Feminine Archetypes in Colette and Marie-Claire Blais." *Journal of the Midwest Modern Language Association* 19.1 (1986): 43-49.
Discusses *Mad Shadows.*

Godard, Barbara. "Blais' *La belle bête*: Infernal Fairy Tale." *Violence in the Canadian Novel Since 1960/dans le roman canadien depuis 1960*. Ed. Virginia Harger-Grinling and Terry Goldie. St. John's, Nfld.: Memorial University, 1981. 159-76.
Discusses *Mad Shadows.*

Gordon, Jan B. "An 'Incandescence of Suffering': The Fiction of Marie-Claire Blais." *Modern Fiction Studies* 22.3 (1976): 467-84.
Overview.

Gould, Karen. "The Censored Word and the Body Politic: Reconsidering the Fiction of Marie-Claire Blais." *Journal of Popular Culture* 15.3 (1981): 14-27.
Overview.

Green, Mary Jean, Paula Gilbert Lewis, and Karen Gould. "Inscriptions of the Feminine: A Century of Women Writing in Quebec." *American Review of Canadian Studies* 15.4 (1985): 363-88.
Discusses *Anna's World.*

Green, Mary Jean. "Redefining the Maternal: Women's Relationships in the Fiction of Marie-Claire Blais." *Traditionalism, Nationalism, and Feminism: Women Writers of Quebec*. Ed. Paula Gilbert Lewis. Westport, CT: Greenwood, 1985. 125-39.
Overview.

Green, Mary Jean. "Structures of Liberation: Female Experience and Autobiographical Form in Quebec." *Yale French Studies* 65 (1983): 124-36.
Discusses *The Manuscripts of Pauline Archange.*

Harris, Michael, trans. Introduction. *Veiled Countries*; *Lives*. By Marie-Claire Blais. Montreal: Vehicule, 1984. 9-10.

Hofsess, John. "'I Am, Simply, a Writer.'" *Books in Canada* Feb. 1979: 8-10.
Interview.

Howells, Coral Ann. "Marie-Claire Blais: *Les Nuits de l'Underground/Nights in the Underground*; Anne Hébert: *Héloïse*." *Private and Fictional Words: Canadian Women Novelists of the 1970s and 1980s*. London: Methuen, 1987. 157-82.

Kattan, Naïm. Introduction. *Mad Shadows*. By Marie-Claire Blais. Trans. Merloyd Lawrence. New Canadian Library 78. Toronto: McClelland and Stewart, 1971. v-x.

Keating, L. Clark. "Marie-Claire Blais, French Canadian Naturalist." *Romance Notes* 15.1 (1973): 10-17.
Overview.

Kertzer, J. M. "*Une Saison dans la vie d'Emmanuel*: A Season in Hell." *Studies in Canadian Literature* 2.2 (1977): 278-88.
Discusses *A Season in the Life of Emmanuel.*

Kraft, James. "Fiction as Autobiography in Quebec: Notes on Pierre Vallières and Marie-Claire Blais." *Novel* 6.1 (1972): 73-78.
Discusses *The Manuscripts of Pauline Archange.*

Kröller, Eva-Marie. "Marie-Claire Blais." *Canadian Writers Since 1960: First Series.* W. H. New. Dictionary of Literary Biography 53. Detroit: Gale, 1986. 66-75.
Overview.

La Bossière, Camille R. "Marie-Claire Blais' *Une Liaison parisienne*: An Ambiguous Discovery of the Old World." *Selecta* 2 (1981): 139-41.
Discusses *A Literary Affair.*

Lecker, Robert A. "The Aesthetics of Deception: Marie-Claire Blais' *A Season in the Life of Emmanuel.*" *Essays on Canadian Writing* 4 (1976): 42-55.

Lennox, John. "*La Scouine*: Influences and Significance." *Studies in Canadian Literature* 5 (1980): 47-62.
Discusses *Mad Shadows.*

Lewis, Paula Gilbert. "From Shattered Reflections to Female Bonding: Mirroring in Marie-Claire Blais's *Visions d'Anna.*" *Québec Studies* 2 (1984): 94-104.
Discusses *Anna's World.*

McClung, Molly G. *Women in Canadian Literature.* Toronto: Fitzhenry and Whiteside, 1977. 50-52, 54.
Overview.

Mitcham, Allison. "The Canadian Matriarch: A Study in Contemporary French and English-Canadian Fiction." *Revue de l'Université de Moncton* 7.1 (1974): 37-42.
Discusses *A Season in the Life of Emmanuel.*

Mitcham, Allison. "Women in Revolt: Anne Hébert's, Marie-Claire Blais' and Claire Martin's Nightmare Vision of an Unjust Society." *Alive Magazine* 3.29 (1973): 13-14.
Discusses *Mad Shadows* and *A Season in the Life of Emmanuel.*

Moss, Jane. "Les Folles du Québec: The Theme of Madness in Quebec Women's Theater." *French Review* 57.5 (1984): 617-24.
Discusses *La Nef des sorcières.*

Moss, Jane. "Menippean Satire and the Recent Quebec Novel." *American Review of Canadian Studies* 15.1 (1985): 59-67.
Discusses *St. Lawrence Blues.*

Moss, Jane. "Women's Theater in Quebec." *Traditionalism, Nationalism, and Feminism: Women Writers of Quebec.* Ed. Paula Gilbert Lewis. Westport, CT: Greenwood Press, 1985. 241-54.
Discusses *La Nef des sorcières.*

Northey, Margot. "Terrible Grotesque: *Mad Shadows.*" *The Haunted Wilderness: The Gothic and Grotesque in Canadian Fiction.* Toronto: University of Toronto Press, 1976. 70-78.

Parker, Douglas H. "The Shattered Glass: Mirror and Illusion in *Mad Shadows.*" *Journal of Canadian Fiction* 2.4 (1973): 68-70.

Rackowski, Cheryl Stokes. *Women by Women: Five Contemporary English and French Canadian Novelists.* Diss. University of Connecticut, 1978.
Discusses *The Fugitive.*

Riggan, Byron. "Lightning on the Literary Landscape." *Saturday Night* 19 Mar. 1960: 14-17.
Discusses *Mad Shadows.*

Russell, George. "Nightmare's Child." *Weekend Magazine* 23 Oct. 1976: 10-13.
Interview.

Serafin, Bruce. "Marie-Claire Blais's *La Belle bête.*" *Essays on Canadian Writing* 7-8 (1977): 63-73.
Discusses *Mad Shadows.*

Shek, Ben-Zion. *Social Realism in the French-Canadian Novel.* Montreal: Harvest House, 1977. 287-90.
Discusses *A Season in the Life of Emmanuel.*

Smith, Donald. "Marie-Claire Blais: Deliverance Through Writing." *Voices of Deliverance: Interviews with Quebec and Acadian Writers.* Trans. Larry Shouldice. Toronto: Anansi, 1984. 129-45.
Interview.

Stephens, Sonya. "Polarisation and Stereotype: The Representation of Woman in Marie-Claire Blais's Visual Novel, *Le Sourd dans la ville*." *British Journal of Canadian Studies* 1.2 (1986): 230-37.
Discusses *Deaf to the City*.

Stratford, Philip. *Marie-Claire Blais*. Toronto: Forum House, 1971.
Overview.

Stratford, Philip. "Portraits of the Artist: Alice Munro and Marie-Claire Blais." *All the Polarities: Comparative Studies in Contemporary Canadian Novels in French and English*. Toronto: ECW Press, 1986. 56-70.
Discusses *A Season in the Life of Emmanuel*.

Tougas, Gérard. *History of French-Canadian Literature*. Trans. Alta Lind Cook. 2nd ed. Toronto: Ryerson Press, 1966. 193-94.
Discusses *The Day is Dark*.

Urbas, Jeanette. "A Fragmented Universe." *From* Thirty Acres *to Modern Times: The Story of French-Canadian Literature*. Toronto: McGraw-Hill Ryerson, 1976. 110-22.
Overview.

Vevaina, Coomie S. "Atomized Lives in Limbo: An Analysis of *Mad Shadows* by Marie-Claire Blais." *Literary Criterion* 22.1 (1987): 41-50.

Waelti-Walters, Jennifer. "Beauty and Madness in M.-C. Blais' *La belle bête*." *Journal of Canadian Fiction* 25-26 (1979): 186-98. Rpt. as "Cinderella and *Mad Shadows* (Blais)" in *Fairy Tales and the Female Imagination*. Montreal: Eden, 1982. 45-57.

Waelti-Walters, Jennifer. "Guilt: The Prison of This World." *Canadian Literature* 88 (1981): 47-51.
Discusses *The Execution*.

Walker, Sandra Cowan. "Marie-Claire Blais." *Profiles in Canadian Literature*. Ed. Jeffrey M. Heath. Toronto: Dundurn Press, 1982. 4: 85-92.
Overview.

Warwick, Jack. "Two Joual Novels and a Dialectic of Violence." *Violence in the Canadian Novel Since 1960/dans le roman canadien depuis 1960*. Ed. Virginia Harger-Grinling and Terry Goldie. St. John's, Nfld.: Memorial University, 1981. 45-57.
Discusses *St. Lawrence Blues.*

Wilson, Edmund. Foreword [*A Season in the Life of Emmanuel*]. *Tamarack Review* 39 (1966): 3-6. Rpt. in *A Season in the Life of Emmanuel.* By Marie-Claire Blais. Trans. Derek Coltman. New York: Farrar, Straus and Giroux, 1966. v-ix.

Wilson, Edmund. *O Canada: An American's Notes on Canadian Culture*. New York: Farrar, Straus and Giroux, 1964. 147-57.
Overview.

BOOK REVIEWS

ANNA'S WORLD/VISIONS D'ANNA, OU LE VERTIGE

Books in Canada Oct. 1985: 36+.
Canadian Book Review Annual (1984): 176.
Canadian Forum May 1985: 31.
Canadian Literature 107 (1985): 137-39.
French Review 57.1 (1983): 132-33.
Quill and Quire Sept. 1982: 59-60.
Quill and Quire Mar. 1985: 75.
Rubicon 6 (1985-86): 204-05.
University of Toronto Quarterly 56.1 (1986): 73-74.
World Literature Today 57.1 (1983): 60.

DAVID STERNE

Books in Canada Oct. 1973: 13-14.
Canadian Fiction Magazine 12 (1974): 95-97.
Journal of Canadian Fiction 3.3 (1974): 105-06.
Quill and Quire Sept. 1973: 7.
Saturday Night Nov. 1973: 53-54.
Tamarack Review 46 (1968): 109-13.
University of Toronto Quarterly 43.4 (1974): 343.

DAY IS DARK, AND THREE TRAVELERS/LE JOUR EST NOIR; LES VOYAGEURS SACRES

American Scholar 36.4 (1967): 708+.
Books in Canada Oct. 1985: 36+.
Canadian Book Review Annual (1985): 206.
Canadian Literature 109 (1986): 110-11.
New York Times Book Review 30 Apr. 1967: 4.
Quill and Quire Mar. 1985: 75.
Saturday Review of Literature 29 Apr. 1967: 29.
Tamarack Review 46 (1968): 109-13.

DEAF TO THE CITY/LE SOURD DANS LA VILLE

Books in Canada Oct. 1981: 29.
Broadside 4 Feb. 1982: 16.
Canadian Book Review Annual (1981): 124-25.
Canadian Literature 117 (1988): 126-32.
French Review 54.4 (1981): 616.
Maclean's 24 Mar. 1980: 56-57.
New York Times Book Review 20 Sept. 1987: 12-13.
Quill and Quire June 1981: 34.
Saturday Night Sept. 1981: 68+.
University of Toronto Quarterly 51.4 (1982): 400-02.
West Coast Review 16.4 (1982): 61-63.
World Literature Today 55.1 (1981): 61-62.

DURER'S ANGEL/LES APPARENCES

Books in Canada Apr. 1977: 25-26.
Canadian Book Review Annual (1976): 152.
Canadian Forum June-July 1977: 58.
Essays on Canadian Writing 7-8 (1977): 26-30.
Fiddlehead 114 (1977): 147-49.
Journal of Canadian Fiction 24 (1979): 134-37.
Matrix 3.1 (1977): 5-6.
Open Letter 3rd ser.8 (1978): 118-20.
Quill and Quire 15 Feb. 1977: 8.
Waves 6.1 (1977): 77-80.

THE EXECUTION/L'EXECUTION

Books in Canada Apr. 1977: 18-19.
Canadian Literature 76 (1978): 101-04.
Quill and Quire 15 Feb. 1977: 8.

THE FUGITIVE/L'INSOUMISE

Canadian Fiction Magazine 32-33 (1979-80): 177-79.
Fiddlehead 121 (1979): 163-64.
Room of One's Own 4.4 (1979): 76-78.
University of Toronto Quarterly 48.4 (1979): 388-90.

A LITERARY AFFAIR/UNE LIAISON PARISIENNE

Branching Out 7.1 (1980): 50-51.
Canadian Book Review Annual (1979): 101.
Fiddlehead 126 (1980): 159-61.
International Fiction Review 5.1 (1978): 66-67.
Quill and Quire Jan. 1980: 25.
Saturday Night Nov. 1979: 39-40.
University of Toronto Quarterly 49.4 (1980): 387.
World Literature Today 51.3 (1977): 412.

MAD SHADOWS/LA BELLE BETE

Canadian Literature 7 (1961): 72-74.
Commonweal 9 Dec. 1960: 297-99.
Dalhousie Review 41.4 (1961-62): 577+.
Times Literary Supplement 17 Mar. 1961: 165.
University of Toronto Quarterly 30.4 (1961): 415-16.

THE MANUSCRIPTS OF PAULINE ARCHANGE/LES MANUSCRITS DE PAULINE ARCHANGE

Commonweal 13 Nov. 1970: 178-80.
New York Review of Books 22 Oct. 1970: 38-42.
New York Times Book Review 12 July 1970: 35.
New Yorker 26 Sept. 1970: 138-42.
Saturday Night Aug. 1970: 25-26.
Tamarack Review 57 (1971): 84-88.

NIGHTS IN THE UNDERGROUND/LES NUITS DE L'UNDERGROUND

Books in Canada Aug.-Sept. 1979: 16.
Branching Out 7.1 (1980): 50-51.
Canadian Book Review Annual (1979): 120-21.
Canadian Fiction Magazine 32-33 (1979-80): 177-79.
Canadian Forum Sept. 1979: 28-29.
Fiddlehead 126 (1980): 159-61.
Fireweed 5-6 (1979-80): 195-96.
French Review 52.6 (1979): 948-49.
Journal of Canadian Studies 14.3 (1979): 142-44.
Queen's Quarterly 87.1 (1980): 161-63.
Quill and Quire July 1978: 41-42.
Quill and Quire July 1979: 49-50.
Saturday Night Sept. 1979: 54+.
University of Toronto Quarterly 49.4 (1980): 387-88.
World Literature Today 53.2 (1979): 248.

PIERRE, LA GUERRE DU PRINTEMPS 81

Women's Review of Books Jan. 1987: 16.

A SEASON IN THE LIFE OF EMMANUEL/UNE SAISON DANS LA VIE D'EMMANUEL

Atlantic Monthly July 1966: 136.
Canadian Literature 31 (1967): 67-69.
Commonweal 7 Oct. 1966: 28.
Maclean's Magazine 6 Aug. 1966: 47.
New York Review of Books 9 June 1966: 21.
New York Times Book Review 21 Aug. 1966: 28-29.
Quill and Quire July 1976: 33.
Saturday Review of Literature 25 June 1966: 26-27.
Times Literary Supplement 30 Mar. 1967: 272.

ST. LAWRENCE BLUES/UN JOUALONAIS, SA JOUALONIE

Books in Canada Nov. 1974: 3-4.
Canadian Literature 67 (1976): 109-12.
Fiddlehead 104 (1975): 128-33.
Journal of Canadian Fiction 19 (1977): 138-40.
Nation 29 Mar. 1975: 374-76.
New Republic 5 Oct. 1974: 23-24.
New York Times Book Review 29 Sept. 1974: 4-5.
New Yorker 24 Mar. 1975: 115-16.
Quill and Quire Dec. 1974: 19.
Quill and Quire Jan. 1975: 23-24.
Times Literary Supplement 14 Mar. 1975: 269.
West Coast Review 10.1 (1975): 57-60.

TETE BLANCHE

Canadian Literature 12 (1962): 65-67.
New York Times Book Review 4 Feb. 1962: 4-5.
Queen's Quarterly 69.3 (1962): 467.
Saturday Night 9 Dec. 1961: 54+.
University of Toronto Quarterly 31.4 (1962): 460.

VEILED COUNTRIES; LIVES/PAYS VOILES; EXISTENCES

Books in Canada Apr. 1985: 29-30.
Canadian Author and Bookman 61.1 (1985): 24.
Canadian Book Review Annual (1984): 215.
Cross-Canada Writers' Quarterly 7.2 (1985): 22.
Fiddlehead 144 (1985): 100-03.
Poetry Canada Review 6.4 (1985): 28.
Quarry 34.2 (1985): 78-80.
Rubicon 5 (1985): 176-78.
University of Toronto Quarterly 54.4 (1985): 393-95.

THE WOLF/LE LOUP

Books in Canada Nov. 1974: 3+.
Canadian Literature 63 (1975): 120-22.
Dalhousie Review 54.4 (1974-75): 786-87.
Fiddlehead 104 (1975): 128-33.
Queen's Quarterly 82.2 (1975): 294-95.
Quill and Quire Oct. 1974: 20.
University of Toronto Quarterly 44.4 (1975): 311.

BOUCHER, DENISE (1935-)

WORKS BY DENISE BOUCHER

Retailles. With Madeleine Gagnon. Montreal: L'Etincelle, 1977.

Cyprine. Montreal: L'Aurore, 1978.

Les Fées ont soif. Montreal: Editions Intermède, 1978. *The Fairies are Thirsty*. Trans. Alan Brown. Vancouver: Talonbooks, 1982.

Lettres d'Italie. Montreal: L'Hexagone, 1987.

WORKS ABOUT DENISE BOUCHER

Dworin, Ruth. "Director, Holly Dennison." *Broadside* July 1981: 14.
Discusses *The Fairies are Thirsty*.

Gould, Karen. "Madeleine Gagnon's Po(e)tical Vision: Portrait of an Artist and an Era." *Traditionalism, Nationalism and Feminism: Women Writers of Quebec*. Ed. Paula Gilbert Lewis. Westport, CT: Greenwood, 1985. 185-204.
Discusses *Retailles*.

Gould, Karen. "Quebec Feminists Look Back: Inventing the Text Through History." *Québec Studies* 1.1 (1983): 298-308.
Discusses *Cyprine*.

Gould, Karen. "Setting Words Free: Feminist Writing in Quebec." *Signs* 6.4 (1981): 617-42.
Discusses *The Fairies are Thirsty*.

Hopkins, Elaine R. "Feminism and a Female Trinity in Denise Boucher's *Les Fées ont soif*." *American Review of Canadian Studies* 14.1 (1984): 63-71.
Discusses *The Fairies are Thirsty*.

Huston, Nancy. "Blasphemy in 'Nouvelle France' Yesterday and Today." *Maledicta* 5.1-2 (1981): 163-69.
Discusses *The Fairies are Thirsty*.

Mezei, Kathy. "The Question of Gender in Translation: Examples from Denise Boucher and Anne Hébert: A Corollary to Evelyne Voldeng's Trans lata latus (*Tessera* No. 1)." *Canadian Fiction Magazine* 57 (1986): 136-41.
Discusses *The Fairies are Thirsty.*

Moss, Jane. "Les Folles du Québec: The Theme of Madness in Québec Women's Theater." *French Review* 57.5 (1984): 617-24.
Discusses *The Fairies are Thirsty.*

Moss, Jane. "Women's Theater in Quebec." *Traditionalism, Nationalism and Feminism: Women Writers of Quebec.* Ed. Paula Gilbert Lewis. Westport, CT: Greenwood, 1985. 241-54.
Discusses *The Fairies are Thirsty.*

Poeteet, Susan H. "An Interview with Denise Boucher." *Fireweed* 5-6 (1979-80): 71-74.

BOOK REVIEWS

THE FAIRIES ARE THIRSTY/LES FEES ONT SOIF

Canadian Literature 117 (1988): 126-32.
Essays on Canadian Writing 30 (1984-85): 304-08.
Fiddlehead 139 (1984): 97-100.
Quill and Quire Apr. 1979: 34.
Quill and Quire Apr. 1983: 26+.
University of Toronto Quarterly 52.4 (1983): 394-95.

BROSSARD, NICOLE (1943-)

WORKS BY NICOLE BROSSARD

"Aube à la saison" in *Trois*. With Michel Beaulieu and Micheline De Jordy. Montreal: Presses de l'A.G.E.U.M., 1965.

Mordre en sa chair. Montreal: Editions Estérel, 1966.

L'Echo bouge beau. Montreal: Editions Estérel, 1968.

Le Centre blanc. Montreal: Editions d'Orphée, 1970.

Un Livre. Montreal: Editions du Jour, 1970. *A Book*. Trans. Larry Shouldice. Toronto: Coach House Press, 1976.

Narrateur et Personnage. Montreal: Radio-Canada, 1970.

Suite logique. Montreal: L'Hexagone, 1970.

Mécanique jongleuse. Colombes, Fr.: Génération, 1973.

Sold-out, étreinte/illustration. Montreal: Editions du Jour, 1973. *Turn of a Pang*. Trans. Patricia Claxton. Toronto: Coach House Press, 1976.

French Kiss: étreinte-exploration. Montreal: Editions du Jour, 1974. *French Kiss, or, A Pang's Progress*. Trans. Patricia Claxton. Toronto: Coach House Press, 1986.

Mécanique jongleuse, suivi de Masculin grammaticale. Montreal: L'Hexagone, 1974. *Daydream Mechanics*. Trans. Larry Shouldice. Toronto: Coach House Press, 1980.

La Partie pour le tout. Montreal: L'Aurore, 1975.

La Nef des sorcières. With Marie-Claire Blais, Marthe Blackburn, Luce Guilbeault, France Théoret, Odette Gagnon and Pol Pelletier. Montreal: Editions Quinze, 1976. *A Clash of Symbols*. Trans. Linda Gaboriau. Toronto: Coach House Press Manuscript Editions, 1979.

L'Amèr: ou, Le Chapitre effrité. Montreal: Quinze, 1977. *These Our Mothers, Or: The Disintegrating Chapter*. Trans. Barbara Godard. Toronto: Coach House Press, 1983.

Le Centre blanc: poèmes 1965-1975. Montreal: L'Hexagone, 1978.

D'arcs de cycle à la dérive. Saint-Jacques-le-Mineur, Que.: Editions de la Maison, 1979.

Les Stratégies du réel: the story so far 6. Ed. Nicole Brossard. Montreal: Nouvelle Barre du Jour; Toronto: Coach House Press, 1979.

Amantes. Montreal: Quinze, 1980. *Lovhers*. Trans. Barbara Godard. Montreal: Guernica, 1986.

Le Sens apparent. Paris: Flammarion, 1980.

Picture theory. Montreal: Nouvelle Optique, 1982.

Double-impression: poèmes et textes 1967-1984. Montreal: L'Hexagone, 1984.

Journal intime, ou, Voilà donc un manuscrit. Montreal: Les Herbes rouges, 1984.

Domaine d'écriture. Montreal: nbj, 1985.

La Lettre aérienne. Montreal: Editions du Remue-ménage, 1985. *The Aerial Letter*. Trans. Marlene Wildeman. Toronto: Women's Press, 1988.

Mauve. With Daphne Marlatt. English and French. Montreal: nbj/writing, 1985.

Dont j'oublie le titre. Marseilles: Editions Ryôan-ji, 1986.

Le Désert mauve. Montreal: L'Hexagone, 1987.

Sous la langue=Under tongue. Trans. Susanne de Lotbinière-Harwood. Montreal: L'Essentielle/Gynergy Books, 1987.

WORKS ABOUT NICOLE BROSSARD

Bayard, Caroline. "Subversion is the Order of the Day." *Essays on Canadian Writing* 7-8 (1977): 17-25.
Overview.

Belleau, Janick. "Women Writers' Contribution to Language." *Contemporary Verse 2* 9.3-4 (1986): 99-103.
Discusses *Women and Words: The Anthology*.

Claxton, Patricia, trans. Translator's Foreword. *French Kiss, or, A Pang's Progress.* By Nicole Brossard. Toronto: Coach House Press, 1986. 5-8.

Cotnoir, Louise, et al. "Interview with Nicole Brossard on *Picture Theory.*" *Canadian Fiction Magazine* 47 (1983): 122-35.

Cotnoir, Louise. "Woman/Women on stage." *A Mazing Space: Writing Canadian Women Writing*. Ed. Shirley Neuman and Smaro Kamboureli. Edmonton: Longspoon, 1986. 307-11.
Discusses *La Nef des sorcières.*

Forsyth, Louise. "Beyond the Myths and Fictions of Traditionalism and Nationalism: The Political in the Work of Nicole Brossard." *Traditionalism, Nationalism, and Feminism: Women Writers of Quebec*. Ed. Paula Gilbert Lewis. Westport, CT: Greenwood, 1985. 157-72.
Overview.

Forsyth, Louise. "Destructuring formal space/accelerating motion in the work of Nicole Brossard." *A Mazing Space: Writing Canadian Women Writing*. Ed. Shirley Neuman and Smaro Kamboureli. Edmonton: Longspoon, 1986. 334-44.
Overview.

Forsyth, Louise. "Errant and Air-Born in the City." *The Aerial Letter*. By Nicole Brossard. Trans. Marlene Wildeman. Toronto: Women's Press, 1988. 9-26.

Forsyth, Louise. "Nicole Brossard and the Emergence of Feminist Literary Theory in Quebec Since 1970." *Gynocritics: Feminist Approaches to Canadian and Quebec Women's Writing*. Ed. Barbara Godard. Toronto: ECW Press, 1987. 211-22.
Overview.

Forsyth, Louise. "The Novels of Nicole Brossard: An Active Voice." *Room of One's Own* 4.1-2 (1978): 30-38.
Overview.

Godard, Barbara. "*L'Amèr* or the Exploding Chapter: Nicole Brossard at the Site of Feminist Deconstruction." *Atlantis* 9.2 (1984): 23-34.
Discusses *These Our Mothers, Or: The Disintegrating Chapter*.

Godard, Barbara. "The Avant-Garde in Canada: *Open Letter* and *La barre du jour*." *Ellipse* 23-24 (1979): 98-113.
Discusses writings in *La barre du jour*.

Godard, Barbara. "Language and Sexual Difference." *Atkinson Review of Canadian Studies* 2.1 (1984): 13-20.
Discusses *These Our Mothers, Or: The Disintegrating Chapter* and *Lovhers*.

Godard, Barbara. "The Language of Difference." *Canadian Forum* June-July 1985: 44-46.
Discusses *These Our Mothers, Or: The Disintegrating Chapter*.

Godard, Barbara. "Nicole Brossard." *Profiles in Canadian Literature*. Ed. Jeffrey M. Heath. Toronto: Dundurn Press, 1986. 6: 121-28.
Overview.

Godard, Barbara, trans. Preface. *Lovhers*. By Nicole Brossard. Montreal: Guernica Editions, 1986. 7-12.

Godard, Barbara, trans. Preface. *These Our Mothers, Or: The Disintegrating Chapter*. By Nicole Brossard. Toronto: Coach House Press, 1983. n. pag.

Godard, Barbara. "Translating and Sexual Difference." *Resources for Feminist Research/Documentation sur la recherche feministe* 13.3 (1984): 13-16.
Discusses *These Our Mothers, Or: The Disintegrating Chapter* and *Lovhers*.

Godard, Barbara. "The Translator as Ventriloquist." *Prism International* 20.3 (1982): 35-36.
Discusses poetry.

Godard, Barbara. "Women Loving Women Writing: Nicole Brossard." *Resources for Feminist Research/Documentation sur la recherche feministe* 12.1 (1983): 20-22.
Overview.

Gould, Karen. "Female Tracings: Writing as Re-Vision in the Recent Works of Louky Bersianik, Madeleine Gagnon, and Nicole Brossard." *American Review of Canadian Studies* 13.2 (1983): 74-89.
Overview.

Gould, Karen. "'Our Bodies in Writing': Quebec Women Writers on the Physicality of the Text." *Degré Second* 7 (1983): 133-50.
Discusses *French Kiss*, *These Our Mothers, Or: The Disintegrating Chapter* and *Lovhers*.

Gould, Karen. "Setting Words Free: Feminist Writing in Quebec." *Signs* 6.4 (1981): 617-42.
Discusses *These Our Mothers, Or: The Disintegrating Chapter* and *La Nef des sorcières*.

Gould, Karen. "Spatial Poetics, Spatial Politics: Quebec Feminists on the City and the Countryside." *American Review of Canadian Studies* 12.1 (1982): 1-9.
Discusses *French Kiss* and *Le Sens apparent*.

Green, Mary Jean, Paula Gilbert Lewis, and Karen Gould. "Inscriptions of the Feminine: A Century of Women Writing in Quebec." *American Review of Canadian Studies* 15.4 (1985): 363-88.
Overview.

Hlus, Carolyn. "Writing womanly: theory and practice." *A Mazing Space: Writing Canadian Women Writing*. Ed. Shirley Neuman and Smaro Kamboureli. Edmonton: Longspoon, 1986. 287-97.
Discusses *These Our Mothers, Or: The Disintegrating Chapter*.

Kröller, Eva-Marie. "Nicole Brossard." *Canadian Writers Since 1960: First Series*. Ed. W. H. New. Dictionary of Literary Biography 53. Detroit: Gale, 1986. 105-09.
Overview.

Moss, Jane. "Les Folles du Québec: The Theme of Madness in Quebec Women's Theater." *French Review* 57.5 (1984): 617-24.
Discusses *La Nef des sorcières.*

Moss, Jane. "Women's Theater in Quebec." *Traditionalism, Nationalism and Feminism: Women Writers of Quebec.* Ed. Paula Gilbert Lewis. Westport, CT: Greenwood, 1985. 241-54.
Discusses *La Nef des sorcières.*

Nemeth, Tünde. "Present? or Re-present?" *Canadian Fiction Magazine* 57 (1986): 82-91.
Discusses *La Nef des sorcières* and "Je vais tourner mon corps et faire semblant de la comparer" in *La nouvelle barre du jour* 136-37 (1984): 149-60.

Neuman, Shirley. "Importing Difference." *A Mazing Space: Writing Canadian Women Writing.* Ed. Shirley Neuman and Smaro Kamboureli. Edmonton: Longspoon, 1986. 392-405.
Discusses *These Our Mothers, Or: The Disintegrating Chapter.*

Notar, Cleo. "Nicole Brossard." *So to Speak: Interviews with Contemporary Canadian Writers.* Ed. Peter O'Brien. Montreal: Vehicule Press, 1987. 122-43.

Rosenfeld, Marthe. "The Development of a Lesbian Sensibility in the Work of Jovette Marchessault and Nicole Brossard." *Traditionalism, Nationalism, and Feminism: Women Writers of Quebec.* Ed. Paula Gilbert Lewis. Westport, CT: Greenwood, 1985. 227-39.
Discusses *These Our Mothers, Or: The Disintegrating Chapter, Le Sens apparent* and *Lovhers.*

Weir, Lorraine. "From picture to hologram: Nicole Brossard's grammar of utopia." *A Mazing Space: Writing Canadian Women Writing.* Ed. Shirley Neuman and Smaro Kamboureli. Edmonton: Longspoon, 1986. 345-52.
Discusses *Picture Theory.*

Wildeman, Marlene, trans. Translator's Introduction. *The Aerial Letter.* By Nicole Brossard. Toronto: Women's Press, 1988. 27-31.

Wilson, Jean. "Nicole Brossard: Fāntasies and Realities." *Broadside* June 1981: 11+. Interview.

BOOK REVIEWS

A BOOK/UN LIVRE

Brick 25 (1986): 41-42.
Essays on Canadian Writing 7-8 (1977): 26-30.
Quill and Quire July 1976: 33.

LE CENTRE BLANC

Canadian Literature 87 (1980): 105-08.

DAYDREAM MECHANICS/MECANIQUE JONGLEUSE

Brick 25 (1986): 41-42.
University of Toronto Quarterly 50.4 (1981): 91-92.

FRENCH KISS, OR A PANG'S PROGRESS/FRENCH KISS: ETREINTE-EXPLORATION

Essays on Canadian Writing 36 (1988): 75-80.
Journal of Canadian Fiction 4.3 (1975): 183-85.
Quill and Quire June 1986: 35-36.
Resources for Feminist Research/Documentation sur la recherche feministe 15.4 (1986-87): 61.
University of Toronto Quarterly 57.1 (1987): 94-95.
Women's Review of Books Jan. 1987: 16.

JOURNAL INTIME, OU, VOILA DONC UN MANUSCRIT

Canadian Literature 106 (1985): 101-04.

LOVHERS/AMANTES

Canadian Book Review Annual (1986): 89.
Malahat Review 82 (1988): 95-96.
Rubicon 10 (1988): 336-39.
Women's Review of Books Jan. 1987: 16.

SOUS LA LANGUE=UNDER TONGUE

Broadside July 1987: 12.
Malahat Review 82 (1988): 95-96.
University of Toronto Quarterly 58.1 (1988): 97-98.

THE STORY SO FAR/LES STRATEGIES DU REEL

Canadian Book Review Annual (1979): 179.
Cross-Canada Writers' Quarterly 3.2-3 (1981): 37-38.
Quill and Quire July 1980: 59.
University of Toronto Quarterly 50.4 (1981): 77-78.

THESE OUR MOTHERS, OR: THE DISINTEGRATING CHAPTER/L'AMER: OU, LE CHAPITRE EFFRITE

Brick 25 (1986): 41-42.
Canadian Book Review Annual (1983): 197.
Canadian Literature 105 (1985): 138-39.
University of Toronto Quarterly 53.4 (1984): 407-09.

TURN OF A PANG/SOLD-OUT, ETREINTE-ILLUSTRATION

Brick 25 (1986): 41-42.

CARRIER, ROCH (1937-)

WORKS BY ROCH CARRIER

Les Jeux incompris. Montreal: Editions Nocturne, 1956.

Cherche tes mots, cherche tes pas. Montreal: Editions Nocturne, 1958.

Jolis deuils: petites tragédies pour adultes. Montreal: Editions du Jour, 1964.

La Guerre, yes sir! Montreal: Editions du Jour, 1968. *La Guerre, Yes Sir!* Trans. Sheila Fischman. Toronto: Anansi, 1970.

Floralie, où es-tu? Montreal: Editions du Jour, 1969. *Floralie, Where Are You?* Trans. Sheila Fischman. Toronto: Anansi, 1971.

La Guerre, yes sir! [play] Montreal: Editions du Jour, 1970.

Il est par là, le soleil. Montreal: Editions du Jour, 1970. *Is it the sun, Philibert?* Trans. Sheila Fischman. Toronto: Anansi, 1972.

L'Aube d'acier. Sherbrooke, Que.: Les Auteurs réunis, 1971.

Le Deux-millième étage. Montreal: Editions du Jour, 1973. *They Won't Demolish Me!* Trans. Sheila Fischman. Toronto: Anansi, 1974.

Floralie. Montreal: Editions du Jour, 1974.

Le Jardin des délices. Montreal: La Presse, 1975. *The Garden of Delights*. Trans. Sheila Fischman. Toronto: Anansi, 1978.

Il n'y a pas de pays sans grand-père. Montreal: Stanké, 1977. *No Country Without Grandfathers*. Toronto: Anansi, 1981.

Les Enfants du bonhomme dans la lune. Montreal: Stanké, 1979. *The Hockey Sweater and Other Stories*. Trans. Sheila Fischman. Toronto: Anansi, 1979. *The Hockey Sweater*. Trans. Sheila Fischman. Montreal: Tundra, 1984.

La Céleste Bicyclette. Montreal: Stanké, 1980.

Les Fleurs vivent-elles ailleurs que sur la terre? Montreal: Stanké, 1980.

Les Voyageurs de l'arc-en-ciel. Montreal: Stanké, 1980.

La Dame qui avait des chaînes aux chevilles. Montreal: Stanké, 1981. *Lady With Chains*. Trans. Sheila Fischman. Toronto: Anansi, 1984.

Le Cirque noir. Montreal: Stanké, 1982.

De l'amour dans la ferraille. Montreal: Stanké, 1984. *Heartbreaks Along the Road*. Trans. Sheila Fischman. Toronto: Anansi, 1987.

Ne faites pas mal à l'avenir. Montreal: Editions Paulines, 1984.

La Fleur et autres personnages. Montreal: Editions Paulines, 1985.

L'Ours et le kangourou. Montreal: Stanké, 1986.

Un Chameau en Jordanie. Montreal: Stanké, 1988.

Prières d'un enfant très très sage. Montreal: Stanké, 1988.

WORKS ABOUT ROCH CARRIER

Abley, Mark. "Heartbreak Road: The Author of *La guerre, yes sir*! Has Written His Best Novel Yet." *Saturday Night* Oct. 1987: 59-62.
Discusses *Heartbreaks Along the Road.*

Amprimoz, Alexandre L. "Between Fantasy and Memory." *Antigonish Review* 37 (1979): 101-04.
Discusses *The Hockey Sweater and Other Stories.*

Amprimoz, Alexandre L. "Four Types of Patriotism in Quebec Letters." *Tamarack Review* 74 (1978): 60-68.
Discusses *No Country Without Grandfathers.*

Amprimoz, Alexandre L. "Roch Carrier's Bicycle." *Antigonish Review* 47 (1981): 91-94.
Discusses *La Céleste Bicyclette.*

Atwood, Margaret. *Survival: A Thematic Guide to Canadian Literature*. Toronto: Anansi, 1972. 206, 220-23.
Discusses *La Guerre, Yes Sir!* and *Is it the sun, Philibert?*

Bailey, Nancy I. "The Corriveau Wake: Carrier's Celebration of Life." *Journal of Canadian Fiction* 1.3 (1972): 43-47.
Discusses *La Guerre, Yes Sir!*

Bond, David J. "Carrier's Fiction." *Canadian Literature* 80 (1979): 120-31.
Overview.

Bond, David J. "The Forces of Life and Death in Roch Carrier's Fiction." *Studies in Twentieth Century Literature* 7.1 (1982): 59-76.
Overview.

Cagnon, Maurice. *The French Novel of Quebec*. Boston: Twayne, 1986. 118-22.
Overview.

Cameron, Donald. "Roch Carrier: You Have to Take Some Risk to Tell the Truth." *Conversations With Canadian Novelists*. Toronto: Macmillan, 1973. Pt. 1: 13-29.
Interview.

Carver, Peter. *A Study Guide to Roch Carrier's* La Guerre, Yes Sir! Toronto: House of Anansi, 1978.

Cogswell, Fred. "The French Canadian Novel and the Problem of Social Change." *Journal of Canadian Fiction* 1.2 (1972): 65-68.
Discusses *La Guerre, Yes Sir!*

Czarnecki, Mark. "A Vision That Transcends Borders." *Maclean's* 24 May 1982: 8b-8c.
Interview.

Darling, Michael. "Reading Carrier's 'The Nun Who Returned to Ireland.'" *Canadian Literature* 104 (1985): 24-33.
Discusses *The Hockey Sweater and Other Stories.*

Dorsinville, Max. *Caliban Without Prospero: Essay on Quebec and Black Literature*. Erin, Ont: Porcépic, 1974. 177-95. Discusses *La Guerre, Yes Sir!*

Fischman, Sheila, trans. Translator's Foreword. *Floralie, Where Are You?* By Roch Carrier. Toronto: Anansi, 1971. n. pag.

Fischman, Sheila, trans. Translator's Foreword. *Is it the sun, Philibert?* By Roch Carrier. Toronto: Anansi, 1972. 1-3.

Fischman, Sheila, trans. Translator's Note. *La Guerre, Yes Sir!* By Roch Carrier. Toronto: Anansi, 1970. 1-3.

Fournier, Georges-V. "Roch Carrier: A Quest for the Authentic." *Ellipse* 4 (1970): 35-42.
Discusses *La Guerre, Yes Sir!*, *Floralie, Where Are You?* and short stories.

Godard, Barbara. "The Oral Tradition and Contemporary Fiction." *Essays on Canadian Writing* 7-8 (1977): 46-62.
Discusses *Floralie, Where Are You?*

Hathorn, Ramon. "The Imaginary World of Roch Carrier." *Canadian Modern Language Review* 31.3 (1975): 196-202.
Overview.

Joyaux, Georges. "Carrier's Trilogy: A Second Look at Quebec's Dark Years." *Essays in Honor of Russel B. Nye*. Ed. Joseph Waldmeir. East Lansing, MI: Michigan State University Press, 1978. 105-28.
Discusses *La Guerre, Yes Sir!*, *Floralie, Where Are You?* and *Is it the sun, Philibert?*

Lennox, John. "Carnivalesque and Parody in *Le jardin des délices*." *Canadian Literature* 112 (1987): 48-58.
Discusses *The Garden of Delights*.

Lennox, John. "Roch Carrier." *Profiles in Canadian Literature*. Ed. Jeffrey M. Heath. Toronto: Dundurn Press, 1986. 6: 41-48.
Overview.

Lennox, John. "*La Scouine*: Influences and Significance." *Studies in Canadian Literature* 5 (1980): 47-62.
Discusses *La Guerre, Yes Sir!*

May, Cedric. *Breaking the Silence: The Literature of Québec."* Birmingham, Eng.: University of Birmingham, Regional Studies Centre, 1981. 58-59, 122-28.
Discusses *No Country Without Grandfathers.*

McHugh, Eileen M. "Involuntary Selective Memory as Underlying Structure in Roch Carrier's *Les Enfants du bonhomme dans la lune.*" *Québec Studies* 1.1 (1983): 268-73.
Discusses *The Hockey Sweater and Other Stories.*

Northey, Margot. "Sportive Grotesque." *Canadian Literature* 70 (1976): 14-22.
Discusses *La Guerre, Yes Sir!*

Northey, Margot. "Sportive Grotesque: *La guerre, yes sir!*" *The Haunted Wilderness: The Gothic and Grotesque in Canadian Fiction.* Toronto: University of Toronto Press, 1976. 79-87.

Rasporich, Beverly. "The Literary Humour of Roch Carrier." *Thalia* 8.1 (1985): 37-49.
Discusses *The Hockey Sweater and Other Stories, They Won't Demolish Me!* and *The Garden of Delights.*

Selinger, Bernie. "*La Guerre, Yes Sir!*: Fusing the Notion with the Passion." *Sphinx* 1.2 (1974): 7-20.

Stratford, Philip. "The Comic Muses: Robert Kroetsch and Roch Carrier." *All the Polarities: Comparative Studies in Contemporary Canadian Novels in French and English.* Toronto: ECW Press, 1986. 71-81.
Discusses *La Guerre, Yes Sir!*

Stratford, Philip. "Roch Carrier." *Canadian Writers Since 1960: First Series.* Ed. W. H. New. Dictionary of Literary Biography 53. Detroit: Gale, 1986. 115-23.
Overview.

Sutherland, Ronald. *Second Image: Comparative Studies in Quebec/Canadian Literature.* Toronto: New Press, 1971. 69-71.
Discusses *La Guerre, Yes Sir!*

Urbas, Jeanette. "A Telescoping of Themes." *From* Thirty Acres *to Modern Times: The Story of French-Canadian Literature*. Toronto: McGraw-Hill Ryerson, 1976. 147-56. Discusses *La Guerre, Yes Sir!*, *Floralie, Where Are You?* and *Is it the sun, Philibert?*

BOOK REVIEWS

FLORALIE, WHERE ARE YOU?/FLORALIE, OU ES-TU?

Canadian Fiction Magazine 2-3 (1971): 98-99.
Canadian Forum June 1971: 36.
Canadian Literature 44 (1970): 88-89.
Quarry 20.3 (1971): 58-60.
Queen's Quarterly 79.4 (1972): 567-69.

THE GARDEN OF DELIGHTS/LE JARDIN DES DELICES

Canadian Book Review Annual (1978): 139.
Canadian Fiction Magazine 30-31 (1979): 226-28.
Canadian Literature 88 (1981): 98-100.
Essays on Canadian Writing 12 (1978): 79-83.
Fiddlehead 126 (1980): 163-66.
Matrix 9 (1979): 72-74.
Quill and Quire June 1978: 43.
University of Toronto Quarterly 48.4 (1979): 384-86.
West Coast Review 13.2 (1978): 54-55.

LA GUERRE, YES SIR!

Antigonish Review 2.1 (1971): 89-90.
Canadian Forum Sept. 1970: 220.
Canadian Literature 40 (1969): 86-87.
Maclean's Magazine June 1970: 77+.
Queen's Quarterly 79.4 (1972): 567-69.
Saturday Night May 1970: 42-43.
Tamarack Review 55 (1970): 88-90.

HEARTBREAKS ALONG THE ROAD/DE L'AMOUR DANS LA FERRAILLE

American Review of Canadian Studies 18.1 (1988): 112-13.
Books in Canada Dec. 1987: 21-22.
Canadian Forum Dec. 1987: 41-42.
Maclean's 2 Nov. 1987: 52f.
Quill and Quire Jan. 1988: 24.
Rubicon 10 (1988): 322-23.
University of Toronto Quarterly 58.1 (1988): 86.

HOCKEY SWEATER

Canadian Book Review Annual (1984): 326.
Canadian Children's Literature 45 (1987): 90-91.
Quarry 34.1 (1985): 91-92.

THE HOCKEY SWEATER AND OTHER STORIES/LES ENFANTS DU BONHOMME DANS LA LUNE

Books in Canada Nov. 1979: 10.
Brick 14 (1982): 59-60.
Canadian Forum Sept. 1979: 30.
Canadian Forum Mar. 1980: 36-37.
Canadian Literature 91 (1981): 131-34.
Fiddlehead 126 (1980): 163-66.
Quill and Quire Apr. 1980: 34.
University of Toronto Quarterly 49.4 (1980): 383-84.
World Literature Today 54.1 (1980): 67.

IS IT THE SUN, PHILIBERT?/IL EST PAR LA, LE SOLEIL

Canadian Fiction Magazine 10 (1973): 98-106.
Canadian Literature 50 (1971): 87-88.
Queen's Quarterly 79.4 (1972): 567-69.
Saturday Night July 1972: 43-44.
University of Toronto Quarterly 42.4 (1973): 354-55.

LADY WITH CHAINS/LA DAME QUI AVAIT DES CHAINES AUX CHEVILLES

Books in Canada Dec. 1984: 28.
Canadian Book Review Annual (1984): 179-80.
Canadian Literature 96 (1983): 147-49.
Canadian Literature 106 (1985): 128-30.
Fiddlehead 145 (1985): 85-88.
Quarry 34.2 (1985): 93-97.
Quill and Quire Mar. 1985: 72.
University of Toronto Quarterly 54.4 (1985): 390.

NO COUNTRY WITHOUT GRANDFATHERS/IL N'Y A PAS DE PAYS SANS GRAND-PERE

Books in Canada Feb. 1982: 9-10.
Canadian Book Review Annual (1981): 127.
French Review 52.5 (1979): 789-90.
University of Toronto Quarterly 51.4 (1982): 393-94.
World Literature Today 52.2 (1978): 249-50.

L'OURS ET LE KANGOUROU

Canadian Literature 115 (1987): 255-57.

THEY WON'T DEMOLISH ME!/LE DEUX-MILLIEME ETAGE

Canadian Forum May-June 1974: 26.
Canadian Literature 63 (1975): 96-98.
Canadian Reader July 1974: 4.
Journal of Canadian Fiction 3.1 (1974): 97-99.
Queen's Quarterly 82.2 (1975): 294-95.
Quill and Quire June 1974: 12.
Saturday Night Aug. 1974: 31.
Time (*Can. ed.*) 17 June 1974: 10.
University of Toronto Quarterly 44.4 (1975): 311.

CONAN, LAURE (1845-1924)

(Pseud. of Félicité Angers)

WORKS BY LAURE CONAN

Angéline de Montbrun. Quebec: Léger Brousseau, 1884. *Angéline de Montbrun*. Trans. Yves Brunelle. Toronto: University of Toronto Press, 1974.

Si les Canadiennes le voulaient! Quebec: C. Darveau, 1886.

A l'oeuvre et à l'épreuve. Quebec: C. Darveau, 1891. *The Master-motive*: *A Tale of the Days of Champlain*. Trans. Theresa A. Gethin. St. Louis, MO: B. Herder, 1909.

Larmes d'amour. Montreal: Leprohon et Leprohon, 1897.

L'Oublié. Montreal: La Revue canadienne, 1900.

Elisabeth Seton. Montreal: La Revue canadienne, 1903.

Une Immortelle. Montreal: La Publicité, 1910.

Jeanne LeBer: *l'adoratrice de Jesus-hostie*. Montreal: Beauchemin, 1910.

Louis Hébert, premier colon du Canada. Quebec: L'Evénement, 1912.

Aux Canadiennes; les Canadiens seront sobres, si vous le voulez. Quebec: Cie d'impr. commerciale, 1913.

Physionomies de saints. Montreal: Beauchemin, 1913.

Silhouettes canadiennes. Quebec: L'Action sociale, 1917.

L'Obscure souffrance. Quebec: L'Action sociale, 1919.

La Vaine foi. Montreal: Imprimerie Maisonneuve, 1921.

La Sève immortelle. Montreal: Bibliothèque de l'Action française, 1925.

Laure Conan. Ed. Micheline Dumont. Montreal: Fides, 1960.

Oeuvres romanesques. 3 vols. Ed. Roger Le Moine. Montreal: Fides, 1974.

WORKS ABOUT LAURE CONAN

Blodgett, E. D. "The Father's seduction: the example of Laure Conan's *Angéline de Montbrun*." *A Mazing Space: Writing Canadian Women Writing*. Ed. Shirley Neuman and Smaro Kamboureli. Edmonton: Longspoon, 1986. 17-30.

Brunelle, Yves, trans. Bibliographical Note. *Angéline de Montbrun*. By Laure Conan. Toronto: University of Toronto Press, 1974. xxviii-xxxiii.

Brunelle, Yves, trans. Introduction. *Angéline de Montbrun*. By Laure Conan. Toronto: University of Toronto Press, 1974. vii-xxvii.

Cagnon, Maurice. *The French Novel of Quebec*. Boston: Twayne, 1986. 13-16.
Discusses *Angéline de Montbrun*.

Dufault, Roseanna. "Personal and Political Childhood in Quebec: Analogies for Identity." *Continental, Latin-American and Francophone Women Writers*. Ed. Eunice Myers and Ginette Adamson. Lanham, MD: UP of America, 1987. 63-69.
Discusses *Angéline de Montbrun*.

Duffy, Dennis. *Sounding the Iceberg: An Essay on Canadian Historical Novels*. Toronto: ECW Press, 1986. 25-27.
Discusses *La Sève immortelle*, *The Master-motive: A Tale of the Days of Champlain* and *L'Oublié*.

Gallays, François. "Reflections in the Pool: The Subtext of Laure Conan's *Angéline de Montbrun*." *Traditionalism, Nationalism, and Feminism: Women Writers of Quebec*. Ed. Paula Gilbert Lewis. Wesport, CT: Greenwood, 1985. 11-26.

Green, Mary Jean, Paula Gilbert Lewis, and Karen Gould. "Inscriptions of the Feminine: A Century of Women Writing in Quebec." *American Review of Canadian Studies* 15.4 (1985): 361-88.
Discusses *Angéline de Montbrun*.

Green, Mary Jean. "Laure Conan and Madame de La Fayette: Rewriting the Female Plot." *Essays on Canadian Writing* 34 (1987): 50-63.
Discusses *Angéline de Montbrun.*

Heidenreich, Rosmarin. "Narrative Strategies in Laure Conan's *Angéline de Montbrun.*" *Canadian Literature* 81 (1979): 37-46.

Roden, Lethem Sutcliffe. *Laure Conan: The First French Canadian Woman Novelist (1845-1924).* Diss. University of Toronto, 1956.
Overview.

Smart, Patricia. "My Father's House: Exploring a Patriarchal Culture." *Canadian Forum* Dec. 1987: 28-35.
Discusses *Angéline de Montbrun.*

Tougas, Gérard. *History of French-Canadian Literature.* Trans. Alta Lind Cook. 2nd ed. Toronto: Ryerson Press, 1966. 52-54.
Overview.

BOOK REVIEWS

ANGELINE DE MONTBRUN

Canadian Book Review Annual (1975): 118-19.
Queen's Quarterly 83.2 (1976): 351-52.
Quill and Quire Aug. 1975: 27.

DUBE, MARCEL (1930-)

WORKS BY MARCEL DUBE

Zone. Montreal: Editions de la Cascade, 1956. *Zone.* Trans. Aviva Ravel. Toronto: Playwrights Canada, 1982.

Le Temps des lilas [suivi de] Un Simple soldat. Quebec: Institut littéraire du Québec, 1958; rev. Montreal: Editions de l'Homme, 1967.

Florence. Quebec: Institut littéraire du Québec, 1960.

Le Train du nord. Montreal: Editions du Jour, 1961.

Les Beaux Dimanches. Montreal: Leméac, 1968.

Bilan. Montreal: Leméac, 1968.

Textes et documents. Montreal: Leméac, 1968.

Au retour des oies blanches. Montreal: Leméac, 1969. *The White Geese.* Trans. Jean Remple. Toronto: New Press, 1972.

Hold-up! With Louis-George Carrier. Montreal: Leméac, 1969.

Pauvre amour. Montreal: Leméac, 1969.

Le Coup de l'étrier et Avant de t'en aller. Montreal: Leméac, 1970.

Entre midi et soir. Montreal: Leméac, 1971.

Un matin comme les autres. Montreal: Leméac, 1971.

Le Naufragé. Montreal: Leméac, 1971.

L'Echéance du vendredi: suivi de Paradis perdu. Montreal: Leméac, 1972.

Médée. Montreal: Leméac, 1972.

La Cellule. Montreal: Leméac, 1973.

De l'autre côté du mur: suivi de cinq courtes pièces. Montreal: Leméac, 1973.

Jérémie: argument de ballet. English and French. Trans. Jean Remple. Montreal: Leméac, 1973.

Manuel. Montreal: Leméac, 1973.

La Tragédie est un acte de foi. Montreal: Leméac, 1973.

L'Impromptu de Québec, ou, Le Testament. Montreal: Leméac, 1974.

Poèmes de sable. Montreal: Leméac, 1974.

Virginie. Montreal: Leméac, 1974.

L'été s'appelle Julie. Montreal: Leméac, 1975.

Dites-le avec des fleurs. With Jean Barbeau. Montreal: Leméac, 1976.

Octobre. Montreal: Leméac, 1977.

Le Réformiste, ou, l'honneur des hommes. Montreal: Leméac, 1977.

L'Amérique à sec. Montreal: Leméac, 1986.

Jean-Paul Lemieux et le livre. Montreal: Art global, 1988.

WORKS ABOUT MARCEL DUBE

Collet, Paulette. "Marcel Dubé." *Profiles in Canadian Literature*. Ed. Jeffrey M. Heath. Toronto: Dundurn Press, 1982. 4: 37-44.
Overview.

Dorsinville, Max. "The Changing Landscape of Drama in Quebec." *Dramatists in Canada: Selected Essays*. Ed. William H. New. Vancouver: University of British Columbia Press, 1972. 179-95.
Discusses *Zone* and *Un Simple soldat*.

Francoeur, Louis. "Quebec Theatre: Stimulation or Communication." *Contemporary Quebec Criticism*. Ed. and trans. Larry Shouldice. Toronto: University of Toronto Press, 1979. 171-94.
Discusses *The White Geese.*

Hamblet, Edwin C. *Marcel Dubé and French-Canadian Drama*. New York: Exposition Press, 1970.
Overview.

Hamblet, Edwin Joseph. "North American Outlook of Marcel Dubé and William Inge." *Queen's Quarterly* 77.3 (1970): 374-87.
Discusses *Le Temps des lilas.*

Hamelin, Jean. *The Theatre in French Canada*. Quebec: Dept. of Cultural Affairs, 1968. 63-67.
Overview.

Johnstone, Ken. "The On- and Offstage Life of a Boy Wonder." *Maclean's Magazine* 22 Nov. 1958: 34-35+.
Overview.

Nardocchio, Elaine. "Structural Analysis of Drama: Practical and Theoretical Implications." *Computers and the Humanities* 19.4 (1985): 221-23.
Discusses *Pauvre amour.*

Nardocchio, Elaine F. "Semiotics and Quebec Theatre - The Case of Marcel Dubé's *Pauvre amour.*" *Kodikas/Code-ARS Semeiotica* 4-5.3-4 (1982): 239-63.

Nardocchio, Elaine F. "Structural Analysis of Drama: A Québécois Example." *Computers in Literary and Linguistic Computing: Proceedings of the Eleventh International Conference*. Paris: Champion-Slatkine, 1985. 267-75.
Discusses *Pauvre amour.*

Nardocchio, Elaine F. *Theatre and Politics in Modern Quebec*. Edmonton: University of Alberta Press, 1986. 41-45.
Overview.

Pagé, Raymond. "Theatre in Quebec." *Chelsea Journal* Mar.-Apr. 1975: 85-94.
Discusses *Zone.*

Remple, Jean, trans. Introduction. *The White Geese*. By Marcel Dubé. Toronto: New Press, 1972. v-vii.

Tougas, Gérard. *History of French-Canadian Literature*. Trans. Alta Lind Cook. 2nd ed. Toronto: Ryerson Press, 1966. 240.
Discusses *Zone*, *Un Simple soldat* and *Le Temps des lilas*.

Usmiani, Renate. "Marcel Dubé." *Canadian Writers Since 1960: First Series*. Ed. W. H. New. Dictionary of Literary Biography 53. Detroit: Gale, 1986. 163-68.
Overview.

Weiss, Jonathan M. *French-Canadian Theater*. Boston: Twayne, 1986. 14-16.
Discusses *Zone* and *The White Geese*.

BOOK REVIEWS

DITES-LE AVEC DES FLEURS

Canadian Theatre Review 18 (1978): 144-45.

OCTOBRE

Canadian Literature 85 (1980): 129-30.

LE REFORMISTE, OU, L'HONNEUR DES HOMMES

Canadian Theatre Review 16 (1977): 93.

THE WHITE GEESE/AU RETOUR DES OIES BLANCHES

Books in Canada Jan.-Feb. 1973: 28.
Canadian Literature 59 (1974): 111-13.
Open Letter 2nd ser.7 (1974): 86-91.
Quill and Quire Feb. 1973: 14.

ZONE

University of Toronto Quarterly 25.2 (1956): 396.

DUCHARME, REJEAN (1941-)

WORKS BY REJEAN DUCHARME

L'Avalée des avalés. Paris: Gallimard, 1966. *The Swallower Swallowed*. Trans. Barbara Bray. London: Hamish Hamilton, 1968.

Le Nez qui voque. Paris: Gallimard, 1967.

L'Océantume. Paris: Gallimard, 1968.

La Fille de Christophe Colomb. Paris: Gallimard, 1969.

L'Hiver de force. Paris: Gallimard, 1973. *Wild to Mild*. Trans. Robert Guy Scully. Saint-Lambert, Que.: Héritage, 1980.

Les Enfantômes. Ottawa: Lacombe; Paris: Gallimard, 1976.

Ines Pérée et Inat Tendu. Montreal: Leméac/Parti pris, 1976.

HA ha!... Saint-Laurent, Que.: Lacombe, 1982. *Ha! Ha!* Trans. David Homel. Toronto: Exile, 1986.

WORKS ABOUT REJEAN DUCHARME

Blouin, Jean, and Jean-Pierre Myette. "In Search of Réjean Ducharme." Trans. Basil Kingstone. *Canadian Fiction Magazine* 47 (1983): 203-12.
Overview.

Bond, D. J. "Search For Identity in the Novels of Réjean Ducharme." *Mosaic* 9.2 (1976): 31-44.
Overview.

Cagnon, Maurice. *The French Novel of Quebec*. Boston: Twayne, 1986. 112-18.
Overview.

Hajdukowski-Ahmed, Maroussia. "The Unique, Its Double and the Multiple: The Carnivalesque Hero in the Québécois Novel." *Yale French Studies* 65 (1983): 139-53.
Discusses *The Swallower Swallowed* and *Le Nez qui voque.*

La Bossière, Camille. "The Dark Age of Enlightenment: Réjean Ducharme's Devilish Children." *The Dark Age of Enlightenment: An Essay on Quebec Literature.* Fredericton, N.B.: York Press, 1980. 39-50.
Discusses *The Swallower Swallowed, Le Nez qui voque* and *L'Océantume.*

La Bossière, Camille R. "Of Renaissance and Solitude in Quebec: A Recollection of the Sixties." *Studies in Canadian Literature* 7.1 (1982): 110-14.
Overview.

Leduc-Park, Renée. "Repetition with a Difference in Réjean Ducharme." Trans. Margaret Gray and Renée Leduc-Park. *Yale French Studies* 65 (1983): 201-13.
Discusses *Wild to Mild.*

Meadwell, Kenneth W. "Réjean Ducharme." *Profiles in Canadian Literature.* Ed. Jeffrey M. Heath. Toronto: Dundurn Press, 1986. 6: 73-80.
Overview.

Pavlovic, Myrianne. "Réjean Ducharme." *Canadian Writers Since 1960: Second Series.* Ed. W. H. New. Dictionary of Literary Biography 60. Detroit: Gale, 1987. 54-59.
Overview.

Rubinger, Catherine. "Violence and Children in *L'Avalée des Avalés.*" *Violence in the Canadian Novel Since 1960/dans le roman canadien depuis 1960.* Ed. Virginia Harger-Grinling and Terry Goldie. St. John's, Nfld.: Memorial University, 1981. 149-58.
Discusses *The Swallower Swallowed.*

Shek, Ben-Zion. *Social Realism in the French-Canadian Novel.* Montreal: Harvest House, 1977. 293-96.
Overview.

Sutherland, Ronald. "Children of the Changing Wind." *Journal of Canadian Studies* 5.4 (1970): 3-11. Rpt. in *Second Image: Comparative Studies in Quebec/Canadian Literature.* Toronto: New Press, 1971. 89-107.
Discusses *The Swallower Swallowed.*

Urbas, Jeanette. "A Fragmented Universe." *From* Thirty Acres *to Modern Times: The Story of French Canadian Literature*. Toronto: McGraw-Hill Ryerson, 1976. 118-19.
Discusses *The Swallower Swallowed.*

Wagg, Heather Elizabeth. *Subject and Text in Réjean Ducharme's* L'Avalée des avalés and Le Nez qui voque. Diss. University of British Columbia, 1985.
Discusses *The Swallower Swallowed* and *Le Nez qui voque.*

Weiss, Jonathan. "The Deadly Games of Réjean Ducharme." *French-Canadian Theater*. Boston: Twayne, 1986. 77-93.
Overview.

Williams, Penny. "Nobody Who Almost Won the Prix Goncourt." *Maclean's Magazine* Jan. 1967: 67.
General.

BOOK REVIEWS

LES ENFANTOMES

Times Literary Supplement 14 May 1976: 578.
World Literature Today 51.2 (1977): 248.

HA! HA!

Books in Canada Mar. 1987: 25.
Canadian Book Review Annual (1987): 193.
French Review 56.6 (1983): 974-75.
University of Toronto Quarterly 57.1 (1987): 88.

INES PEREE ET INAT TENDU

Canadian Theatre Review 22 (1979): 114.

FERRON, JACQUES (1921-1985)

WORKS BY JACQUES FERRON

L'Ogre. Montreal: Cahiers de la File Indienne, 1949.

La Barbe de François Hertel; Le Licou. Montreal: Editions d'Orphée, 1951.

Le Dodu; ou le prix du bonheur. Montreal: Editions d'Orphée, 1956.

Tante Elise; ou le prix de l'amour. Montreal: Editions d'Orphée, 1956.

Le Cheval de Don Juan. Montreal: Editions d'Orphée, 1957. Rev. as *Le Don Juan Chrétien* in *Théâtre*. Vol. One. Montreal: Déom, 1968.

Les Grands Soleils. Montreal: Editions d'Orphée, 1958. *The Flowering Suns*. Trans. Julie Stockton. M.A. Thesis. York University, 1983.

Corolles. Paris: Grassin, 1961.

Contes du pays incertain. Montreal: Editions d'Orphée, 1962.

Cotnoir. Montreal: Editions d'Orphée, 1962. *Dr. Cotnoir*. Trans. Pierre Cloutier. Montreal: Harvest House, 1973.

La Tête du roi. Montreal: A.G.E.U.M., 1963.

Cazou; ou le prix de la virginité. Montreal: Editions d'Orphée, 1964.

Contes anglais et autres. Montreal: Editions d'Orphée, 1964.

La Nuit. Montreal: Parti Pris, 1965. Rev. as *Les Confitures de coings* in *Les Confitures de coings et autres textes*. Montreal: Parti Pris, 1972. Trans. in *Quince Jam*. Trans. Ray Ellenwood. Toronto: Coach House Press, 1977.

Papa Boss. Montreal: Parti Pris, 1966. Rev. in *Les Confitures de coings et autres textes*. Montreal: Parti Pris, 1972. Trans. in *Quince Jam*. Trans. Ray Ellenwood. Toronto: Coach House Press, 1977.

La Charrette. Montreal: HMH, 1968. *The Cart*. Trans. Ray Ellenwood. Toronto: Exile, 1980.

Contes - Edition intégrale: *Contes anglais*, *Contes du pays incertain*, *Contes inédits*. Montreal: HMH, 1968. *Tales from the Uncertain Country*. Trans. Betty Bednarski. Toronto: Anansi, 1972. *Selected Tales of Jacques Ferron*. Trans. Betty Bednarski. Toronto: Anansi, 1984.

Théâtre. Vol. One. Montreal: Déom, 1968.

Le Ciel de Québec. Montreal: Editions du Jour, 1969. *The Penniless Redeemer*. Trans. Ray Ellenwood. Toronto: Exile, 1984.

Historiettes. Montreal: Editions du Jour, 1969.

L'Amélanchier. Montreal: Editions du Jour, 1970. *The Juneberry Tree*. Trans. Raymond Y. Chamberlain. Toronto: Harvest House, 1975.

Le Salut de l'Irlande. Montreal: Editions du Jour, 1970.

Les Roses sauvages; petit roman suivi d'une lettre d'amour soigneusement présentée. Montreal: Editions du Jour, 1971. *Wild Roses: A Story Followed by a Love Letter*. Trans. Betty Bednarski. Toronto: McClelland and Stewart, 1976.

La Chaise du maréchal ferrant. Montreal: Editions du Jour, 1972.

Les Confitures de coings et autres textes. Montreal: Parti Pris, 1972. *Quince Jam*. Trans. Ray Ellenwood. Toronto: Coach House Press, 1977.

Le Saint-Elias. Montreal: Editions du Jour, 1972. *The Saint Elias*. Trans. Pierre Cloutier. Montreal: Harvest House, 1975.

Du fond de mon arrière-cuisine. Montreal: Editions du Jour, 1973.

Escarmouches: La Longue Passe. 2 vols. Montreal: Leméac, 1975.

Théâtre. Vol. Two. Montreal: Déom, 1975.

Les Confitures de coings et autres textes, suivi de Le Journal des confitures de coings. Rev. and enl. Montreal: Parti Pris, 1977.

Gaspé-Mattempa. Trois-Rivières, Que.: Editions du Bien Public, 1980.

Rosaire, précédé de L'Exécution de Maski. Montreal: VLB, 1981.

La Conférence inachevée. Montreal: VLB, 1987.

WORKS ABOUT JACQUES FERRON

Atwood, Margaret. *Survival: A Thematic Guide to Canadian Literature.* Toronto: Anansi, 1972. 229-30.
Discusses "Cadieu" from *Tales from the Uncertain Country.*

Bartlett, Brian. "Les Nouvelles de Cousin Emmanuel: Varieties of Salvation and Imagination in Ferron's *Cotnoir.*" *Studies in Canadian Literature* 12.2 (1987): 177-86.
Discusses *Dr. Cotnoir.*

Bednarski, Betty, trans. Afterword. *Wild Roses: A Story Followed by a Love Letter.* By Jacques Ferron. Toronto: McClelland and Stewart, 1976. 120-23.

Bednarski, Betty, trans. Introduction. *Selected Tales of Jacques Ferron.* By Jacques Ferron. Toronto: Anansi, 1984. 11-16.

Bednarski, Betty, trans. Introduction. *Tales from the Uncertain Country.* By Jacques Ferron. Toronto: House of Anansi, 1972. i-v.

Bednarski, Betty. "Jacques Ferron (1921-1985)." *Canadian Literature* 107 (1985): 193-95.
Obituary.

Bednarski, Betty. "Jacques Ferron." *Profiles in Canadian Literature*. Ed. Jeffrey M. Heath. Toronto: Dundurn Press, 1986. 5: 121-28.
Overview.

Bednarski, Betty. "Rereading Jacques Ferron." *Antigonish Review* 61 (1985): 43-49.
Overview.

Bourassa, André G. *Surrealism and Quebec Literature*. Trans. Mark Czarnecki. Toronto: University of Toronto Press, 1984. 198-200.
Overview.

Bruineman, Margaret. "Rhinos' Farewell." *Maclean's* 13 May 1985: 20.
General.

Cagnon, Maurice. *The French Novel of Quebec*. Boston: Twayne, 1986. 84-90.
Overview.

Duffy, Dennis. "Of Tales and Novels." *Idler* 5 (1985): 40-43.
Discusses *Selected Tales of Jacques Ferron.*

Duffy, Dennis. *Sounding the Iceberg: An Essay on Canadian Historical Novels*. Toronto: ECW Press, 1986. 59.
Discusses *The Penniless Redeemer.*

Ellenwood, Ray. "Death and Dr. Ferron." *Brick* 24 (1985): 6-9.
Overview.

Ellenwood, Ray. "Goliath and the Prix David." *Brick* 4 (1978): 55-56.
General.

Ellenwood, Ray. "How Not to Quince Words: A Translator Reflects on Jacques Ferron, the Political Doctor Who Writes With a Scalpel." *Books in Canada* May 1976: 8-11.
Overview.

Ellenwood, Ray. Introduction [to Special Issue on Jacques Ferron]. *Brick* 16 (1982): 4-5.

Ellenwood, Ray. "Morley Callaghan, Jacques Ferron, and the Dialectic of Good and Evil." *The Callaghan Symposium*. Ed. David Staines. Ottawa: University of Ottawa Press, 1981. 37-46.
Discusses "Archangel of the Suburbs" from *Tales from the Uncertain Country*, *Saint-Elias* and *The Penniless Redeemer*.

Ellenwood, Ray, trans. Translator's Afterword. *The Penniless Redeemer*. By Jacques Ferron. Toronto: Exile, 1984. 339-42.

Ellenwood, Ray, trans. Translator's Notes. *The Cart*. By Jacques Ferron. Toronto: Exile, 1980. 139-44.

Hamelin, Jean. *The Theatre in French Canada*. Quebec: Dept. of Cultural Affairs, 1968. 70-71.
General.

May, Cedric. "Canadian Writing: Beautiful Losers in Presqu'Amérique." *Bulletin of Canadian Studies* 3.2 (1979): 5-18.
Overview.

Nardocchio, Elaine. "Structural Analysis of Drama: Practical and Theoretical Implications." *Computers and the Humanities* 19.4 (1985): 221-23.
Discusses *The Flowering Suns*.

Nardocchio, Elaine F. "Structural Analysis of Drama: A Québécois Example." *Computers in Literary and Linguistic Computing: Proceedings of the Eleventh International Conference*. Paris: Champion-Slatkine, 1985. 267-75.
Discusses *The Flowering Suns*.

Sarkar, Eileen. "The Uncertain Countries of Jacques Ferron and Mordecai Richler." *Canadian Fiction Magazine* 13 (1974): 98-107.
Discusses *Tales from the Uncertain Country*.

Schleser, Jörg-Peter. "Schizophrenic Uncertainties: The Quiet Revolutions of Hugh Hood and Jacques Ferron." *Journal of Canadian Culture* 2.2 (1985): 109-23.
Overview.

Shek, Ben-Zion. *Social Realism in the French-Canadian Novel*. Montreal: Harvest House, 1977. 237-45.
Discusses *Dr. Cotnoir*.

Smith, Donald. "Jacques Ferron: The Marvellous Folly of Writing." *Voices of Deliverance: Interviews with Quebec and Acadian Writers*. Trans. Larry Shouldice. Toronto: Anansi, 1986. 83-103.
Interview.

St. Pierre, Paul Matthew. "Jacques Ferron." *Canadian Writers Since 1960: Second Series*. Ed. W. H. New. Dictionary of Literary Biography 60. Detroit: Gale, 1987. 64-74.
Overview.

Urbas, Jeanette. "The 'New' Novel: Revolt in Literature." *From* Thirty Acres *to Modern Times: The Story of French-Canadian Literature*. Toronto: McGraw-Hill Ryerson, 1976. 125-34.
Discusses *Dr. Cotnoir*.

Verthuy, Mair E., and Jennifer Waelti-Walters. "Critical Practice and the Transmission of Culture." *Neohelicon* 14.2 (1987): 405-14.
Discusses *La Nuit*.

Weiss, Jonathan. *French-Canadian Theater*. Boston: Twayne, 1986. 139-46.
Discusses *The Flowering Suns* and *La Tête du roi*.

Ziroff, Mary. *A Study Guide to Jacques Ferron's* Tales from the Uncertain Country. Toronto: Anansi, 1977.

BOOK REVIEWS

THE CART/LA CHARRETTE

Books in Canada Feb. 1982: 14-15.
Canadian Book Review Annual (1981): 132-33.
University of Toronto Quarterly 51.4 (1982): 399-400.

LA CONFERENCE INACHEVEE

Books in Canada Jan.-Feb. 1988: 21-22.

DR. COTNOIR/COTNOIR

Books in Canada Jan. 1975: 8-9.
Canadian Fiction Magazine 16 (1975): 101-04.
Chelsea Journal Mar.-Apr. 1979: 78-79.
Journal of Canadian Fiction 3.2 (1974): 107-08.
Saturday Night Feb. 1974: 34.

ESCARMOUCHES

Canadian Literature 82 (1979): 118-20.

THE JUNEBERRY TREE/L'AMELANCHIER

Books in Canada Oct. 1975: 21.
Canadian Book Review Annual (1975): 100.
Canadian Fiction Magazine 24-25 (1977): 167-70.
Chelsea Journal Mar.-Apr. 1976: 83-85.
Essays on Canadian Writing 4 (1976): 76-77.
Journal of Canadian Fiction 17-18 (1976): 312-14.
Queen's Quarterly 84.2 (1977): 336-37.
Quill and Quire Oct. 1975: 17.
Tamarack Review 68 (1976): 90-93.
University of Toronto Quarterly 45.4 (1976): 324.

L'OGRE

University of Toronto Quarterly 20.4 (1951): 389-90.

THE PENNILESS REDEEMER/LE CIEL DE QUEBEC

Canadian Book Review Annual (1984): 184.
Quill and Quire June 1985: 40.
University of Toronto Quarterly 56.1 (1986): 74-76.

QUINCE JAM/LES CONFITURES DE COINGS ET AUTRES TEXTES

Brick 4 (1978): 53-54.
Canadian Book Review Annual (1977): 124.
Canadian Literature 82 (1979): 115-18.

THE SAINT ELIAS/LE SAINT-ELIAS

Books in Canada Jan. 1975: 8-9.
Canadian Book Review Annual (1975): 111-12.
Canadian Fiction Magazine 24-25 (1977): 167-70+.
Chelsea Journal Mar.-Apr. 1976: 83-85.
Journal of Canadian Fiction 2.4 (1973): 93-94.
Queen's Quarterly 83.2 (1976): 349-51.
Quill and Quire Oct. 1975: 17.
Tamarack Review 68 (1976): 90-93.

SELECTED TALES OF JACQUES FERRON/CONTES - EDITION INTEGRALE

Books in Canada Dec. 1984: 28.
Canadian Book Review Annual (1984): 184.
Canadian Literature 108 (1986): 166-69.
Matrix 20 (1985): 72-75.
Rubicon 6 (1985-86): 168-69.
University of Toronto Quarterly 54.4 (1985): 389-90.
Waves 14.3 (1986): 92-93.

TALES FROM THE UNCERTAIN COUNTRY/CONTES - EDITION INTEGRALE

Books in Canada June 1972: 9-10.
Canadian Fiction Magazine 11 (1973): 75-77.
Canadian Forum June 1972: 41-42.
Canadian Literature 55 (1973): 124-25.
Dalhousie Review 52.3 (1972): 494-96.
Fiddlehead 110 (1976): 134-37.
Open Letter 2nd ser.3 (1972): 93-97.
Quarry 22.2 (1973): 70-71.
University of Toronto Quarterly 42.4 (1973): 355.

WILD ROSES/LES ROSES SAUVAGES

Canadian Book Review Annual (1976): 138-39.
Canadian Forum Oct. 1976: 33-34.
Canadian Literature 82 (1979): 118-20.
Quill and Quire 15 Apr. 1976: 7.
Saturday Night Nov. 1976: 58-61.

GARNEAU, HECTOR DE SAINT-DENYS (1912-1943)

WORKS BY HECTOR DE SAINT-DENYS GARNEAU

Regards et jeux dans l'espace. Montreal: s.n., 1937.

Poésies complètes - Regards et jeux dans l'espace, Les solitudes. Ed. Robert Elie and Jean Le Moyne. Montreal: Fides, 1949. *Complete Poems of Saint-Denys Garneau*. Trans. John Glassco. Ottawa: Oberon Press, 1975.

Journal. Ed. Robert Elie and Jean Le Moyne. Montreal: Beauchemin, 1954. *The Journal of Saint-Denys Garneau*. Trans. John Glassco. Toronto: McClelland and Stewart, 1962.

St-Denys Garneau and Anne Hébert. Trans. F. R. Scott. Vancouver: Klanak Press, 1962.

Lettres à ses amis. Montreal: Editions HMH, 1967.

Oeuvres. Ed. Jacques Brault and Benoît Lacroix. Montreal: Presses de l'Université de Montréal, 1971.

WORKS ABOUT HECTOR DE SAINT-DENYS GARNEAU

Bourassa, André G. *Surrealism and Quebec Literature*. Trans. Mark Czarnecki. Toronto: University of Toronto Press, 1984. 33-38.
Discusses *Complete Poems*.

Chamberland, Paul. "Founding the Territory." *Contemporary Quebec Criticism*. Ed. and trans. Larry Shouldice. Toronto: University of Toronto Press, 1979. 122-60.
Discusses *Complete Poems*.

Dobbs, Bryan Griffith. *A Critical Edition of Hector de Saint-Denys Garneau's* Regards et jeux dans l'espace. Diss. University of Wisconsin, 1970.
Discusses *Complete Poems*.

Fisette, Jean. "The Question of Enunciation in Poetry: Saint-Denys Garneau." Trans. Christine von Aesch. *Essays on Canadian Writing* 12 (1978): 216-34.
General.

Glassco, John, trans. Introduction. *Complete Poems of Saint-Denys Garneau.* By Hector de Saint-Denys Garneau. Ottawa: Oberon Press, 1975. 5-17.

Haeck, Philippe. "Figures, Summaries, Questions." Trans. Andrea Moorhead. *Ellipse* 37 (1987): 6-15.
Discusses *Oeuvres.*

Hayne, David M. "Forest of Symbols: An Introduction to Saint-Denys Garneau." *Canadian Literature* 3 (1960): 5-16.
Overview.

La Bossière, Camille R. "Affair de culture et non de création: Hector de Saint-Denys Garneau on Classicism." *Classical Models in Literature.* Ed. Zoran Konstantinovic, Warren Anderson, and Walter Dietze. Innsbruck: Instituts für Sprachwissenschaft der Universität Innsbruck, 1981. 55-58.
Overview.

La Bossière, Camille R. "Moi, dédoublement: An Introduction to Hector de Saint-Denys Garneau." *The Dark Age of Enlightenment: An Essay on Quebec Literature.* Fredericton, N.B.: York Press, 1980. 9-15.
Overview.

LeMoyne, Jean. "Saint-Denys Garneau's Testimony for His Times." *Convergence: Essays from Quebec.* Trans. Philip Stratford. Toronto: Ryerson Press, 1966. 199-220.
Overview.

LeMoyne, Jean. "Saint-Denys Garneau's Testimony to His Times." Trans. Philip Stratford. *Canadian Literature* 28 (1966): 31-46.
General.

Mandel, Eli. "Saint-Denys Garneau: Transcending Nationality." *The Family Romance.* Winnipeg, Man.: Turnstone Press, 1986. 147-53.
Discusses *Complete Poems.*

Marcotte, Gilles. Introduction. *The Journal of Saint-Denys Garneau.* By Hector de Saint-Denys Garneau. Trans. John Glassco. Toronto: McClelland and Stewart, 1962. 9-15.

May, C. R. P. "Saint-Denys Garneau: A Canadian Catholic Reader of Mauriac in the 1930's." *Literature and Society: Studies in Nineteenth and Twentieth Century French Literature Presented to R. J. North.* Ed. C. A. Burns. Birmingham: Goodman for University of Birmingham, 1980. 193-99.
Discusses *The Journal.*

May, Cedric. *Breaking the Silence: The Literature of Québec.* Birmingham, Eng.: University of Birmingham, Regional Studies Centre, 1981. 62-63, 72-74.
Discusses poetry.

May, Cedric. "Self and Non-Self: The Sense of Otherness in Quebec Poetry." *Bulletin of Canadian Studies* 2.2 (1978): 52-63.
Discusses poetry.

Merler, Grazia. "Translation and the Creation of Cultural Myths in Canada." *West Coast Review* 11.2 (1976): 26-30+.
Discusses *Complete Poems.*

Sanger, Peter, trans. "Saint-Denys Garneau on Poetry, Writing, Painting and Music." *Antigonish Review* 64 (1986): 79-89.
Discusses extracts from his poetry and *The Journal.*

Sylvestre, Guy. "Saint-Denys Garneau's World of Spiritual Communion." Trans. W. E. Collin. *Canadian Poetry Magazine* Mar. 1943: 5-11.
Discusses *Complete Poems.*

Tougas, Gérard. *History of French-Canadian Literature.* Trans. Alta Lind Cook. 2nd ed. Toronto: Ryerson Press, 1966. 196-99.
Discusses *Complete Poems.*

BOOK REVIEWS

COMPLETE POEMS OF SAINT-DENYS GARNEAU/POESIES COMPLETES

Brick 2 (1978): 52-54.
Canadian Book Review Annual (1975): 148.
Canadian Forum Aug. 1976: 39-40.
Canadian Literature 71 (1976): 83-87.
Contemporary Verse 2 2.1 (1976): 18-20.
Quarry 25.4 (1976): 76-80.
Queen's Quarterly 83.4 (1976): 694-95.
Quill and Quire Nov. 1975: 30.
Times Literary Supplement 14 May 1976: 590.
University of Toronto Quarterly 7.4 (1938): 554.

THE JOURNAL OF SAINT-DENYS GARNEAU/JOURNAL

Canadian Author and Bookman 38.4 (1963): 11.
Canadian Forum Aug. 1963: 115-16.
Canadian Literature 17 (1963): 67-68.
Dalhousie Review 43.3 (1963): 427+.
University of Toronto Quarterly 24.3 (1955): 321-24.

OEUVRES

Times Literary Supplement 7 Apr. 1972: 399.

ST-DENYS GARNEAU AND ANNE HEBERT

British Columbia Library Quarterly 26.3 (1963): 29+.
Canadian Forum Dec. 1962: 210.
Queen's Quarterly 70.3 (1963): 449-50.
Tamarack Review 29 (1963): 80-82.

GAUVREAU, CLAUDE (1925-1971)

WORKS BY CLAUDE GAUVREAU

"L'Ombre sur le cerceau. Au coeur des quenouilles. Bien être." *Refus global*. Montreal: Mithra-Mythe, 1948.

Sur fil métamorphose. Montreal: Erta, 1956.

Brochuges. Montreal: Editions Feu-Antonin, 1957.

Etal mixte. Montreal: Editions d'Orphée, 1968.

Oeuvres créatrices complètes. Montreal: Parti Pris, 1977.

Entrails. Trans. Ray Ellenwood. Toronto: Coach House Press, 1981.

WORKS ABOUT CLAUDE GAUVREAU

Bourassa, André G. "The Poetic Design of Claude Gauvreau." Trans. Christine von Aesch. *Essays on Canadian Writing* 9 (1977-78): 70-82.
Discusses *Oeuvres créatrices complètes.*

Bourassa, André G. *Surrealism and Quebec Literature*. Toronto: University of Toronto Press, 1984. passim.
Overview.

Duguay, Raoul. "Poetry is Yrteop: Interview/Conversation." Trans. David Lobdell. *Ellipse* 17 (1975): 80-97.

Ellenwood, Ray. "The Automatic Translator." *Prism International* 20.3 (1982): 37-39.
Discusses *Entrails.*

Ellenwood, Ray. "The Automatist Movement of Montreal: Towards Non-Figuration in Painting." *Canadian Literature* 113-114 (1987): 11-27.
Discusses *Oeuvres créatrices complètes.*

Ellenwood, Ray, trans. Introduction and Translator's Note. *Entrails*. By Claude Gauvreau. Toronto: Coach House Press, 1981. 7-18.

Ellenwood, W. R. "Surrealism and the 'Automatistes' of Montreal." *Actes du VIIe congrès de l'Association Internationale de Littérature comparée/Proceedings of the 7th Congress of the International Comparative Literature Association*. Ed. Milan V. Dimic and Juan Ferraté. Stuttgart: Bieber, 1979. 1: 257-59.
Overview.

Ferron, Jacques. "Claude Gauvreau." Trans. Ray Ellenwood. *Exile* 3.2 (1975): 20-57.
Biographical.

Shek, Ben. "Quebec Letter: Le Théâtre du nouveau monde." *Performing Arts* 9.3 (1972): 44-45.
Discusses *Les Oranges sont vertes*.

Weiss, Jonathan M. *French-Canadian Theater*. Boston: Twayne, 1986. 19-22.
Discusses *Les Oranges sont vertes* and *Le Coureur de marathon*.

BOOK REVIEWS

ENTRAILS

Canadian Book Review Annual (1981): 182.
University of Toronto Quarterly 51.4 (1982): 398-99.

GELINAS, GRATIEN (1909-)

WORKS BY GRATIEN GELINAS

Tit-Coq. Montreal: Beauchemin, 1949. *Tit-Coq*. Trans. Kenneth Johnstone and Gratien Gélinas. Toronto: Clarke, Irwin, 1967.

Bousille et les Justes. Quebec: Institut littéraire du Québec, 1960. *Bousille and The Just*. Trans. Kenneth Johnstone. Toronto: Clarke, Irwin, 1961.

Hier, les enfants dansaient. Montreal: Leméac, 1968. *Yesterday the Children Were Dancing*. Trans. Mavor Moore. Toronto: Clarke, Irwin, 1967.

Les Fridolinades, 1945 et 1946. Montreal: Quinze, 1980.

Les Fridolinades, 1943 et 1944. Montreal: Quinze, 1981.

Les Fridolinades, 1941 et 1942. Montreal: Quinze, 1981.

La Passion de Narcisse Mondoux. Montreal: Leméac, 1987.

Les Fridolinades, 1938, 1939, 1940. Montreal: Leméac, 1988.

WORKS ABOUT GRATIEN GELINAS

Béraud, Jean. "Theatre in French Canada." *The Arts in Canada: A Stocktaking at Mid-Century*. Ed. Malcolm Ross. Toronto: Macmillan, 1958. 161-62.
Discusses *Tit-Coq* and *Les Fridolinades.*

"[*Bousille and the Just*]." *Canadian Drama/L'art dramatique canadien* 11.1 (1985): 26-29. Rpt. in *Canadian Drama and the Critics*. Ed. L. W. Conolly. Vancouver: Talonbooks, 1987. 36-40.
Selections from newspaper and periodical reviews and articles.

Clark, J. Wilson. "Gélinas' Propaganda for Reformism and Terrorism in Quebec." *Literature and Ideology* 14 (1972): 43-50.
Discusses *Yesterday the Children Were Dancing*.

Coulter, John. "Fridolin Plans a Show with English Idiom." *Saturday Night* 18 Jan. 1947: 3.
Discusses *Les Fridolinades*.

Cox, Carolyn. "Fridolin, the Bright French Star That Canada Has 'Discovered.'" *Saturday Night* 14 Apr. 1945: 2.
Discusses *Les Fridolinades*.

Gélinas, Gratien. "Credo of the Comédie-Canadienne: The Faith Behind the Little Miracle." *Queen's Quarterly* 66.1 (1959): 18-25.
About theatre.

Gélinas, Gratien ("Fridolin"). "Why Broadway Turned Me Down." *Saturday Night* 6 Mar. 1951: 8+.
Discusses *Tit-Coq*.

Hamelin, Jean. *The Theatre in French Canada*. Quebec: Dept. of Cultural Affairs, 1968. 57-60.
Discusses *Tit-Coq* and *Bousille and the Just*.

Johnstone, K. "Fridolin... + Gratien Gélinas = Two-Way Success." *Canadian Business* Mar. 1950: 36-38+.
Discusses *Tit-Coq*.

"Laughter and Tears." Rev. of *Tit-Coq* by Gratien Gélinas. *Time* (*Can. ed.*) 10 Jan. 1949: 13.

LeCocq, Thelma. "The Great Fridolin." *Maclean's Magazine* 1 Feb. 1945: 7+.
Biographical.

Lefolii, Ken. "Visit With Gratien Gélinas." *Maclean's Magazine* 30 Jan. 1960: 22-23+.
General.

Moore, Mavor. "Gratien Gélinas." *4 Canadian Playwrights*. Toronto: Holt, Rinehart and Winston, 1973. 32-39.
Overview.

Nardocchio, Elaine F. *Theatre and Politics in Modern Quebec*. Edmonton: University of Alberta Press, 1986. 28-30, 34-37.
Overview.

Nathan, George Jean. "Ti-Coq." *Theatre Book of the Year, 1950-51: A Record and An Interpretation*. New York: Knopf, 1951. 217-18.
Discusses *Tit-Coq*.

Ness, Margaret. "'Little Rooster' Flies the Coop." Rev. of *Tit-Coq* by Gratien Gélinas. *Saturday Night* 28 Nov. 1950: 10.

Pagé, Raymond. "Theatre in Quebec." *Chelsea Journal* Mar.-Apr. 1975: 85-94.
Discusses *Tit-Coq*.

Primeau, Marguerite A. "Gratien Gélinas and His Heroes." *British Columbia Library Quarterly* 26.4 (1963): 13-19.
Discusses *Tit-Coq* and *Bousille and the Just*.

Riggan, Byron. "Montreal." *Tamarack Review* 13 (1959): 104-06.
Discusses *Bousille and the Just*.

Robertson, George Hillyard. "Riches for the Little Rooster." *Maclean's Magazine* 15 Nov. 1950: 10-11+.
General.

Sabbath, Lawrence. "Gratien Gélinas Speaks Out on Canadian Playwrights." *Performing Arts in Canada* 2.3 (1963): 27.
Interview.

Stewart, Mrs. Carl. "DDF Report." *Performing Arts in Canada* 2.4 (1964): 37-44.
Interview.

Taaffe, Gerald. "Gratien and the Terrorists: A Middle-Aged Playwright Looks at Separatism With a Young Man's Eyes." Rev. of *Yesterday the Children Were Dancing* by Gratien Gélinas. *Maclean's Magazine* 2 July 1966: 45-46.

Tougas, Gérard. *History of French-Canadian Literature*. Trans. Alta Lind Cook. 2nd ed. Toronto: Ryerson Press, 1966. 239.
Discusses *Tit-Coq* and *Bousille and the Just*.

Usmiani, Renate. *Gratien Gélinas*. Toronto: Gage Educational Publishing, 1977.
Overview.

Usmiani, Renate. "The Playwright as Historiographer: New Views of the Past in Contemporary Quebec Drama." *Canadian Drama/L'art dramatique canadien* 8.2 (1982): 117-28.
Discusses *Les Fridolinades.*

Von Vusen, Lisa. "Gratien Gélinas: A Legend on the Stage." *Maclean's* 5 Sept. 1988: 8b-8c.
Discusses *The Passion of Narcisse Mondoux.*

Walker, E. A. "Gratien Gélinas." *Profiles in Canadian Literature.* Ed. Jeffrey M. Heath. Toronto: Dundurn Press, 1982. 3: 89-96.
Overview.

Weiss, Jonathan. *French-Canadian Theater.* Boston: Twayne, 1986. 9-14.
Overview.

Woloch, Michael. "The Playwright of St. Tite and the Poet of St. Dilom." *French Review* 38.2 (1964): 191-95.
Discusses *Tit-Coq* and *Bousille and the Just.*

BOOK REVIEWS

BOUSILLE AND THE JUST/BOUSILLE ET LES JUSTES

University of Toronto Quarterly 31.4 (1962): 490-91.

FRIDOLINADES, 1941 ET 1942, 1943 ET 1944

Canadian Literature 99 (1983): 103-05.

TIT-COQ

University of Toronto Quarterly 20.4 (1951): 388-89.

GODBOUT, JACQUES (1933-)

WORKS BY JACQUES GODBOUT

Carton-pâte. Paris: Seghers, 1956.

Les Pavés secs. Montreal: Beauchemin, 1958.

C'est la chaude loi des hommes. Montreal: Editions de l'Hexagone, 1960.

L'Aquarium. Paris: Seuil, 1962.

Le Couteau sur la table. Paris: Seuil, 1965. *Knife on the Table*. Trans. Penny Williams. Toronto: McClelland and Stewart, 1968.

Salut Galarneau! Paris: Seuil, 1967. *Hail Galarneau*! Trans. Alan Brown. Don Mills, Ont.: Longman Canada, 1970.

La Grande Muraille de Chine. With John Robert Colombo. Montreal: Editions du Jour, 1969.

D'Amour, P.Q. Montreal: Editions Hurtubise HMH; Paris: Seuil, 1972.

L'Interview: texte radiophonique. With Pierre Turgeon. Montreal: Leméac, 1973.

Le Réformiste: textes tranquilles. Montreal: Quinze, 1975.

L'Isle au dragon. Paris: Seuil, 1976. *Dragon Island*. Trans. David Ellis. Don Mills, Ont.: Musson, 1978.

Les Têtes à Papineau. Paris: Seuil, 1981.

Le Murmure Marchand, 1976-1984. Montreal: Boréal Express, 1984.

Souvenirs Shop: poèmes et prose 1956-1960. Montreal: Editions de l'Hexagone, 1984.

Une Histoire américaine. Paris: Seuil, 1986.

WORKS ABOUT JACQUES GODBOUT

Bond, David. "Jacques Godbout and the Nature of Reality." *Journal of Canadian Fiction* 31-32 (1981): 203-17.
Overview.

Brown, Alan, trans. Translator's Foreword. *Hail Galarneau*! By Jacques Godbout. Don Mills, Ont.: Longman, 1970. n. pag.

Cagnon, Maurice. *The French Novel of Quebec*. Boston: Twayne, 1986. 74-84.
Overview.

Davies, Gillian. Introduction. *Knife on the Table*. By Jacques Godbout. Trans. Penny Williams. New Canadian Library 130. Toronto: McClelland and Stewart, 1976. vi-xiii.

Dorsinville, Max. *Caliban Without Prospero: Essay on Quebec and Black Literature*. Erin, Ont.: Porcépic, 1974. 177-95.
Discusses *Knife on the Table*.

Falardeau, Jean Charles. "The Evolution of the Hero in the Quebec Novel." *Contemporary Quebec Criticism*. Ed. and trans. Larry Shouldice. Toronto: University of Toronto Press, 1979. 95-116.
Discusses *L'Aquarium*, *Knife on the Table* and *Hail Galarneau*!

Hodgson, Richard G. "Jacques Godbout." *Canadian Writers Since 1960: First Series*. Ed. W. H. New. Dictionary of Literary Biography 53. Detroit: Gale, 1986. 214-18.
Overview.

May, Cedric. *Breaking the Silence: The Literature of Québec*. Birmingham, Eng.: University of Birmingham, Regional Studies Centre, 1981. 99-101.
Discusses *Hail Galarneau*!

May, Cedric. "Canadian Writing: Beautiful Losers in Presqu'Amérique." *Bulletin of Canadian Studies* 3.2 (1979): 5-18.
Discusses *Knife on the Table* and *Hail Galarneau*!

Pivato, Joseph. "Nouveau roman canadien." *Canadian Literature* 58 (1973): 51-60.
Discusses *Knife on the Table*.

Raoul, Valerie. "Documents of Non-Identity: The Diary Novel in Quebec." *Yale French Studies* 65 (1983): 187-200.
Discusses *Hail Galarneau*!

Sénécal, André. "Pepsi Agonistes: Jacques Godbout's Anti-Hero." *French Review* 54.3 (1981): 445-52.
Discusses *Knife on the Table*, *Hail Galarneau*! and *Dragon Island*.

Shek, Ben-Zion. *Social Realism in the French-Canadian Novel*. Montreal: Harvest House, 1977. 273-78.
Discusses *L'Aquarium* and *Knife on the Table*.

Smith, Donald. "Jacques Godbout: Transforming Reality." *Voices of Deliverance*: *Interviews with Quebec and Acadian Writers*. Trans. Larry Shouldice. Toronto: Anansi, 1986. 147-75.
Interview.

Sutherland, Ronald. "The Fourth Separatism." *Canadian Literature* 45 (1970): 7-23.
Discusses *Knife on the Table*.

Sutherland, Ronald. *Second Image*: *Comparative Studies in Quebec/Canadian Literature*. Toronto: New Press, 1971. 16-24, 120-22.
Discusses *Knife on the Table*.

Sutherland, Ronald. "Twin Solitudes." *Canadian Literature* 31 (1967): 5-24.
Discusses *Knife on the Table*.

Tougas, Gérard. *History of French-Canadian Literature*. Trans. Alta Lind Cook. 2nd ed. Toronto: Ryerson Press, 1966. 192.
Discusses *L'Aquarium*.

Urbas, Jeanette. "From Individual Revolt to Social Revolution." *From* Thirty Acres *to Modern Times*: *The Story of French-Canadian Literature*. Toronto: McGraw-Hill Ryerson, 1976. 135-46.
Discusses *Knife on the Table* and *Hail Galarneau*!

Vautier, Marie. "Fiction, Historiography, and Myth: Jacques Godbout's *Les Têtes à Papineau* and Rudy Wiebe's *The Scorched-Wood People*." *Canadian Literature* 110 (1986): 61-78.

Winterburn, Mike. "'Américanité' in Two Recent Quebec Novels." *British Journal of Canadian Studies* 3.2 (1988): 277-84.
Discusses *Une Histoire américaine.*

BOOK REVIEWS

D'AMOUR, P.Q.

Canadian Literature 62 (1974): 114-15.
Times Literary Supplement 20 Oct. 1972: 1245.

DRAGON ISLAND/L'ISLE AU DRAGON

Books in Canada Apr. 1979: 8.
Canadian Literature 86 (1980): 119-20.
French Review 51.2 (1977): 328-29.
Quill and Quire Jan. 1977: 21.
Tamarack Review 71 (1977): 82-90.
University of Toronto Quarterly 49.4 (1980): 393-94.
World Literature Today 51.4 (1977): 591.

HAIL GALARNEAU!/SALUT GALARNEAU!

Canadian Fiction Magazine 2-3 (1971): 99-100.
Canadian Literature 49 (1971): 87-88.
Saturday Night Dec. 1970: 38.
Tamarack Review 57 (1971): 84-88.

KNIFE ON THE TABLE/LE COUTEAU SUR LA TABLE

British Columbia Library Quarterly 32.2 (1968): 23-24.
Canadian Forum July 1968: 94.
Fiddlehead 76 (1968): 90-91.
Quill and Quire Apr. 1976: 40.

LES TETES A PAPINEAU

Canadian Literature 96 (1983): 111-13.
Quill and Quire Mar. 1982: 64.
Times Literary Supplement 15 Jan. 1982: 63.
World Literature Today 57.1 (1983): 67.

GRANDBOIS, ALAIN (1900-1975)

WORKS BY ALAIN GRANDBOIS

Né à Québec. Paris: Messein, 1933. *Born in Quebec*. Trans. Evelyn M. Brown. Montreal: Palm, 1964.

Poèmes. Hankéou: Chine, 1934.

Les Voyages de Marco Polo. Montreal: Bernard Valiquette, 1941.

Les îles de la nuit. Montreal: Parizeau, 1944.

Avant le chaos. Montreal: Editions Modernes, 1945. *Champagne & Opium*. Trans. Larry Shouldice. Montreal: Quadrant Editions, 1984.

Rivages de l'homme. Quebec: n.p., 1948.

L'Etoile pourpre. Montreal: L'Hexagone, 1957.

Alain Grandbois. Ed. Jacques Brault. Montreal: Fides, 1958.

Poèmes: *Les îles de la nuit*, *Rivages de l'homme*, *L'Etoile pourpre*. Montreal: L'Hexagone, 1963.

Selected Poems. Trans. Peter Miller. Toronto: Contact Press, 1964.

Alain Grandbois. Ed. Jacques Brault. Montreal: L'Hexagone, 1968.

Poèmes choisis. Montreal: Fides, 1970.

Visages du monde. Images et souvenirs de l'entre-deux guerres. Montreal: Editions Hurtubise HMH, 1971.

Délivrance du jour et autres inédits. Montreal: Editions du Sentier, 1980.

Poèmes inédits. Montreal: Presses de l'Université de Montréal, 1985.

Lettres à Lucienne et deux poèmes inédits. Montreal: L'Hexagone, 1987.

WORKS ABOUT ALAIN GRANDBOIS

Beaver, John. "Alain Grandbois: A Final Note." *Journal of Canadian Fiction* 4.1 (1975): 144-45.
Biographical.

Beaver, John. "The Prose of Alain Grandbois: The Landscape of an Apprentice-Poet." *Journal of Canadian Fiction* 4.1 (1975): 136-43.
Overview.

Bourassa, André G. *Surrealism and Quebec Literature.* Trans. Mark Czarnecki. Toronto: University of Toronto Press, 1984. 54-57.
Discusses *Les Iles de la nuit*, *Rivages de l'homme* and *L'Etoile pourpre.*

DesRochers, Alfred, et al. "Extracts from *Liberté*: Critical Appraisals of Alain Grandbois." *Ellipse* 14-15 (1974): 69-79.
Discusses poetry.

Lacourcière, Luc. Foreword. *Born in Quebec.* By Alain Grandbois. Trans. Evelyn M. Brown. Montreal: Palm, 1964. n. pag.

May, Cedric. "Alain Grandbois: Benighted Prometheus *Bulletin of Canadian Studies* 8.2 (1984): 111-19.
Discusses poetry.

May, Cedric. *Breaking the Silence: The Literature of Québec.* Birmingham, Eng.: University of Birmingham, Regional Canadian Studies Centre, 1981. 74-79.
Discusses *Les Iles de la nuit.*

May, Cedric. "Form and Structure in *Les Iles de la nuit* by Alain Grandbois." *Gaining Ground: European Critics on Canadian Literature.* Ed. Robert Kroetsch and Reingard M. Nischik. Western Canadian Literary Documents 6. Edmonton: NeWest, 1985. 192-204.

May, Cedric. "Self and Non-Self: The Sense of Otherness in Quebec Poetry." *Bulletin of Canadian Studies* 2.2 (1978): 52-63.
Discusses poetry.

Miller, Peter, trans. "Alain Grandbois." *Selected Poems*. By Alain Grandbois. Toronto: Contact Press, 1964. ix-xi.

Tougas, Gérard. *History of French-Canadian Literature*. Trans. Alta Lind Cook. 2nd ed. Toronto: Ryerson Press, 1966. 177, 199-201.
Overview.

Warwick, Jack. *The Long Journey: Literary Themes of French Canada*. Toronto: University of Toronto Press, 1968. 60-62.
Discusses *Born in Quebec*.

BOOK REVIEWS

BORN IN QUEBEC/NE A QUEBEC

Canadian Literature 30 (1966): 72-73.

CHAMPAGNE AND OPIUM/AVANT LE CHAOS

Rubicon 6 (1985-86): 208-09.
University of Toronto Quarterly 56.1 (1986): 74.

SELECTED POEMS

Books Abroad 39 (1965): 383.
Canadian Author and Bookman 40.3 (1965): 14.
Canadian Forum July 1965: 95.
Canadian Literature 30 (1966): 72.
Poetry Apr. 1966: 50-51.

GUEVREMONT, GERMAINE (1893-1968)

WORKS BY GERMAINE GUEVREMONT

En pleine terre. Montreal: Editions Paysana, 1942; enl. Montreal: Paysana, 1946.

Le Survenant. Montreal: Beauchemin, 1945. *The Outlander*. Trans. Eric Sutton. Toronto: McGraw-Hill, 1950. Republished as *Monk's Reach*. Trans. Eric Sutton. London: Evans, 1950.

Marie-Didace. Montreal: Beauchemin, 1947; rev. Montreal: Beauchemin, 1948. *The Outlander*. Trans. Eric Sutton. Toronto: McGraw-Hill, 1950. Republished as *Monk's Reach*. Trans. Eric Sutton. London: Evans, 1950.

WORKS ABOUT GERMAINE GUEVREMONT

Benazon, Michael. "Germaine Guèvremont." *Canadian Writers, 1920-1959: First Series*. Ed. W. H. New. Dictionary of Literary Biography 68. Detroit: Gale, 1988. 160-63.
Overview.

Cagnon, Maurice. *The French Novel of Quebec*. Boston: Twayne, 1986. 31-34.
Discusses *The Outlander*.

Green, Mary Jean. "Gabrielle Roy and Germaine Guèvremont: Quebec's Daughters Face a Changing World." *Journal of Women's Studies in Literature* 1.3 (1979): 243-57.
Discusses *The Outlander*.

Herlan, James J. "*Le Survenant* as Ideological Messenger: A Study of Germaine Guèvremont's Radio Serial." *Traditionalism, Nationalism, and Feminism: Women Writers of Quebec*. Ed. Paula Gilbert Lewis. Westport, CT: Greenwood, 1985. 37-51.
Discusses *The Outlander*.

May, Cedric. *Breaking the Silence: The Literature of Québec.* Birmingham, Eng.: University of Birmingham, Regional Studies Centre, 1981. 50-53.
Discusses *The Outlander.*

Mollica, Anthony. "Imagery and Internal Monologue in *Le Survenant.*" *Canadian Modern Language Review* 25.1 (1968): 5-11.
Discusses *The Outlander.*

Mollica, Anthony. Introduction. *The Outlander.* By Germaine Guèvremont. Trans. Eric Sutton. New Canadian Library 151. Toronto: McClelland and Stewart, 1978. v-vx.

Tougas, Gérard. *History of French-Canadian Literature.* Trans. Alta Lind Cook. 2nd ed. Toronto: Ryerson Press, 1966. 131-32.
Overview.

Urbas, Jeanette. "Undermining the Myth." *From* Thirty Acres *to Modern Times: The Story of French-Canadian Literature.* Toronto: McGraw-Hill Ryerson, 1976. 25-31.
Discusses *The Outlander.*

van Lent, Peter. "Absence and Departure: The Male Mystique in French-Canadian Literature Before 1950." *American Review of Canadian Studies* 16.1 (1986): 17-23.
Discusses *The Outlander.*

Williamson, Richard C. "The Stranger Within: Sexual Politics in the Novels of Germaine Guèvremont." *Québec Studies* 1.1 (1983): 246-56.
Discusses *The Outlander.*

"You Asked Us." *Canadian Magazine* 21 May 1977: 19.
General.

BOOK REVIEWS

THE OUTLANDER/LE SURVENANT; MARIE-DIDACE

Commonweal 31 Mar. 1950: 659.
Nation 17 June 1950: 602-03.
New York Times Book Review 5 Mar. 1950: 6.
Quill and Quire Apr. 1978: 36.
Saturday Night 28 Mar. 1950: 21.
Saturday Review of Literature 18 Mar. 1950: 14.
Time (*Can. ed.*) 13 Mar. 1950: 62-63.
University of Toronto Quarterly 15.4 (1946): 411-12.
University of Toronto Quarterly 17.4 (1948): 405.

HEBERT, ANNE (1916-)

WORKS BY ANNE HEBERT

Les Songes en équilibre. Montreal: Editions de l'Arbre, 1942.

Le Torrent. Montreal: Beauchemin, 1950; enl. ed. Montreal: HMH, 1963. *The Torrent: Novellas and Short Stories*. Trans. Gwendolyn Moore. Montreal: Harvest House, 1973.

Le Tombeau des rois. Quebec: Institut littéraire du Québec, 1953. *The Tomb of the Kings*. Trans. Peter Miller. Toronto: Contact Press, 1967.

Les Chambres de bois. Paris: Editions du Seuil, 1958. *The Silent Rooms*. Trans. Kathy Mezei. Don Mills, Ont.: Musson, 1974.

Poèmes. Paris: Editions du Seuil, 1960. *Poems*. Trans. Alan Brown. Don Mills, Ont.: Musson, 1975.

St-Denys Garneau and Anne Hébert. Trans. F. R. Scott. Vancouver: Klanak Press, 1962.

Le Temps sauvage; suivi de La Mercière assassinée, et Les Invités au procès. Montreal: HMH, 1967. "Les Invités au procès" translated as "The Guests on Trial: A Dramatic Poem for Radio." Trans. Eugene Benson and Renate Benson. *Canadian Drama/L'art dramatique canadien* 9.1 (1983): 165-94.

Dialogue sur la traduction: à propos du 'Tombeau des rois.' With Frank Scott. Montreal: HMH, 1970.

Kamouraska. Paris: Editions du Seuil, 1970. *Kamouraska*. Trans. Norman Shapiro. Don Mills, Ont.: Musson, 1973.

Les Enfants du Sabbat. Paris: Editions du Seuil, 1975. *Children of the Black Sabbath*. Trans. Carol Dunlop-Hébert. Don Mills, Ont.: Musson, 1977.

Héloïse. Paris: Editions du Seuil, 1980. *Héloïse*. Trans. Sheila Fischman. Toronto: Stoddart, 1982.

Les Fous de Bassan. Paris: Editions du Seuil, 1982. *In the Shadow of the Wind*. Trans. Sheila Fischman. Toronto: Stoddart, 1983.

Anne Hébert: Selected Poems. Trans. A. Poulin, Jr. Brockport, NY: BOA Editions, 1987.

Le Premier Jardin. Paris: Editions du Seuil, 1988.

WORKS ABOUT ANNE HEBERT

Amprimoz, Alexandre L. "Four Writers and Today's Quebec." *Tamarack Review* 70 (1977): 72-80.
Discusses *Children of the Black Sabbath.*

Amprimoz, Alexandre L. "Survival Disguised as Metaphysics: Anne Hébert's *Héloïse*." *Waves* 10.4 (1982): 73-75.

Belcher, Margaret. "[*Les fous de Bassan/In the Shadow of the Wind*]." *Canadian Literature* 109 (1986): 159-65.

Benson, Renate. "Aspects of Love in Anne Hébert's Short Stories." *Journal of Canadian Fiction* 25-26 (1979): 160-74.

Benson, Renate. "Character and Symbol in Anne Hébert's 'Les Invités au procès.'" *Canadian Drama/L'art dramatique canadien* 6.1 (1980): 22-29.
Discusses "The Guests on Trial."

Blodgett, E. D. "Prisms and Arcs: Structures in Hébert and Munro." *Figures in a Ground: Canadian Essays on Modern Literature Collected in Honour of Sheila Watson*. Ed. Diane Bessai and David Jackel. Saskatoon: Western Producer Prairie, 1978. 99-121. Rpt. in *Configuration: Essays in the Canadian Literatures*. By E. D. Blodgett. Downsview, Ont.: ECW Press, 1982. 53-84.
Overview.

Boak, Denis. "*Kamouraska, Kamouraska*." *Essays in French Literature* 14 (1977): 69-104.

Brazeau, J. Raymond. "Anne Hébert." *An Outline of Contemporary French Canadian Literature*. Toronto: Forum House, 1972. 59-74.
Discussses *The Torrent*, *The Tomb of the Kings* and *The Silent Rooms.*

Cagnon, Maurice. *The French Novel of Quebec*. Boston: Twayne, 1986. 59-67.
Overview.

Chamberland, Paul. "Founding the Territory." *Contemporary Quebec Criticism*. Ed. and trans. Larry Shouldice. Toronto: University of Toronto Press, 1979. 122-60.
Discusses *Poems*.

Chartier, Armand. "French-Canadian Gothic: Notes on Anne Hébert's *Kamouraska*." *ACSUS Newsletter* 11.2 (1972): 66-75.

Chiasson, Arthur Paul. *The Tragic Moods in the Works of Anne Hébert*. Diss. Tufts University, 1974.
Overview.

Cohen, Henry. "The Role of Myth in Anne Hébert's *Kamouraska*." Trans. Chitra Reddin. *Essays on Canadian Writing* 10 (1978): 134-43.

Cohen, Matt. "Queen in Exile: Though Now One of Canada's Best Known Writers, Anne Hébert Still Bears the Scars of a Long Literary Apprenticeship." *Books in Canada* Aug.-Sept. 1983: 9-12.
Interview.

Collie, Joanne. "Anne Hébert's 'Ecriture féminine.'" *British Journal of Canadian Studies* 3.2 (1988): 285-92.
Overview.

Collin, W. E. "The Poetry of a Dissolving Society." *Canadian Modern Language Review* 11.2 (1955): 9-12.
Discusses *Les Songes en équilibre* and *The Tomb of the Kings*.

Davidson, Arnold E. "Canadian Gothic and Anne Hébert's *Kamouraska*." *Modern Fiction Studies* 27.2 (1981): 243-54.

Davidson, Arnold E. "Rapunzel in *The Silent Rooms*: Inverted Fairy Tales in Anne Hébert's First Novel." *Colby Library Quarterly* 19.1 (1983): 29-36.

Duffy, Dennis. *Sounding the Iceberg*: *An Essay on Canadian Historical Novels*. Toronto: ECW Press, 1986. 54-57.
Discusses *Kamouraska*.

Emmanuel, Pierre. Preface. *The Tomb of the Kings*. By Anne Hébert. Trans. Peter Miller. Toronto: Contact, 1967. 13.

Ewing, Ronald. "Griffin Creek: The English World of Anne Hébert." *Canadian Literature* 105 (1985): 100-10.
Discusses *In the Shadow of the Wind*.

Farley, T. E. *Exiles and Pioneers: Two Visions of Canada's Future 1825-1975*. Ottawa: Borealis, 1976. 119, 125-26, 130, 132.
Discusses *Poems*.

Frye, Northrop. Foreword. *Dialogue sur la traduction: à propos du* Tombeau des rois. By Anne Hébert and Frank Scott. Montreal: HMH, 1970. 11-14.
Discusses *The Tomb of the Kings*.

Garrett, Elaine Hopkins. "Intentionality and Representation in Anne Hébert's *Kamouraska*." *Québec Studies* 6 (1988): 92-103.

Godard, Barbara. "My (m)Other, My Self: Strategies for Subversion in Atwood and Hébert." *Essays on Canadian Writing* 26 (1983): 13-44.
Discusses *Kamouraska*.

Godin, Jean Cléo. "Rebirth in the Word." *Yale French Studies* 45 (1970): 137-53.
Overview of poetry.

Gould, Karen. "Absence and Meaning in Anne Hébert's *Les Fous de Bassan*." *French Review* 59.6 (1986): 921-30.
Discusses *In the Shadow of the Wind*.

Green, Mary Jean. "The Witch and the Princess: The Feminine Fantastic in the Fiction of Anne Hébert." *American Review of Canadian Studies* 15.2 (1985): 137-46.
Discusses *The Silent Rooms*, *Children of the Black Sabbath* and *Kamouraska*.

Hamelin, Jean. *The Theatre in French Canada*. Quebec: Dept. of Cultural Affairs, 1968. 75.
Discusses *Le Temps sauvage*.

Harger-Grinling, V., and A. R. Chadwick. "History Reinterpreted: Hébert's *Kamouraska* and Bourin's *Très Sage Héloïse*." *Neohelicon* 14.2 (1987): 151-58.

Hebért, Anne, and Frank Scott. "The Art of Translation." *Tamarack Review* 24 (1962): 65-90.
Discusses *The Tomb of the Kings.*

Howells, Coral Ann. "Marie-Claire Blais: *Les Nuits de l'Underground/Nights in the Underground*; Anne Hébert: *Héloïse.*" *Private and Fictional Words: Canadian Women Novelists of the 1970s and 1980s.* London: Methuen, 1987. 157-82.

Kröller, Eva-Marie. "La Lampe dans la fenêtre: The Visualization of Quebec Fiction." *Canadian Literature* 88 (1981): 74-82.
Discusses *Kamouraska.*

Kröller, Eva-Marie. "Repetition and Fragmentation: A Note on Anne Hébert's *Kamouraska.*" *Literary Half-Yearly* 24.2 (1983): 125-33.

Lecker, Robert. "The Rooms of *Kamouraska.*" *Waves* 4.1 (1975): 14-21.

Lennox, John. "Dark Journeys: *Kamouraska* and *Deliverance.*" *Essays on Canadian Writing* 12 (1978): 84-104.

Lennox, John. "The Past: Themes and Symbols of Confrontation in *The Double Hook* and 'Le Torrent.'" *Journal of Canadian Fiction* 2.1 (1973): 70-72.
Discusses *The Torrent.*

Lennox, John. "*La Scouine*: Influences and Significance." *Studies in Canadian Literature* 5 (1980): 47-62.
Discusses *The Torrent.*

Macri, Francis M. "Anne Hébert: Story and Poem." *Canadian Literature* 58 (1973): 9-18.
Discusses *The Torrent* and *Poems.*

Macri, Francis M. "Not Simply a Problem of Cahin-Caha." *Laurentian University Review/Revue de l'Université Laurentienne* 7.1 (1974): 86-93.
Discusses *The Torrent.*

May, Cedric. "French-Canada's Dissenting Voices." *Bulletin of Canadian Studies* 1.1 (1977): 15-26.
Overview.

McClung, Molly G. *Women in Canadian Literature.* Toronto: Fitzhenry and Whiteside, 1977. 48-50, 54.
Overview.

McDonald, Marci. "Anne Hébert: Charting the Rage Within." *City Woman* (Spring 1981): 54-61+.
Interview.

McDonald, Marci. "Woman Is Not for Taming." *Maclean's* 17 Oct. 1983: 62+.
Interview.

Merivale, Patricia. "Framed Voices: The Polyphonic Elegies of Hébert and Kogawa." *Canadian Literature* 116 (1988): 68-82.
Discusses *In the Shadow of the Wind.*

Merler, Grazia. "Translation and the Creation of Cultural Myths in Canada." *West Coast Review* 11.2 (1976): 26-30+.
Discusses *The Silent Rooms.*

Mezei, Kathy. "Anne Hébert: A Pattern Repeated." *Canadian Literature* 72 (1977): 29-40.
Discusses *The Silent Rooms.*

Mezei, Kathy. "The Question of Gender in Translation: Examples from Denise Boucher and Anne Hébert: A Corollary to Evelyne Voldeng's Trans lata latus (*Tessera* No. 1)." *Canadian Fiction Magazine* 57 (1986): 136-41.
Discusses poetry.

Mitcham, Allison. "Women in Revolt: Anne Hébert's, Marie-Claire Blais' and Claire Martin's Nightmare Visions of an Unjust Society." *Alive Magazine* 3.29 (1973): 13-14.
Discusses *The Torrent* and *Kamouraska.*

Northey, Margot. "Psychological Gothic: *Kamouraska.*" *The Haunted Wilderness: The Gothic and Grotesque in Canadian Fiction.* Toronto: University of Toronto Press, 1976. 53-61.

Pallister, Janis L. "Orphic Elements in Anne Hébert's *Héloïse.*" *Québec Studies* 5 (1987): 125-34.

Paterson, Janet. "Anne Hébert." *Canadian Modern Language Review* 37.2 (1981): 207-11.
Discusses *The Silent Rooms*, *Kamouraska* and *Children of the Black Sabbath.*

Paterson, Janet M. "Anne Hébert." *Profiles in Canadian Literature*. Ed. Jeffrey M. Heath. Toronto: Dundurn Press, 1982. 3: 113-120.
Overview.

Paterson, Janet M. "Anne Hébert and the Discourse of the Unreal." *Yale French Studies* 65 (1983): 172-86.
Discusses *The Silent Rooms*.

Poulin, A., trans. Afterword. "[Anne Hébert - Poems]." *Quarterly Review of Literature: Poetry Series* 21.3-4 (1980): 58-60.

Poulin, Jr., A., trans. "Poetry and the Landscape of Epiphany: On Translating the Poetry of Anne Hébert." *Anne Hébert: Selected Poems*. By Anne Hébert. Brockport, NY: BOA Editions, 1987. 149-57.

Purcell, Patricia. "The Agonizing Solitude: The Poetry of Anne Hébert." *Canadian Literature* 10 (1961): 51-61.
General.

Rackowski, Cheryl Stokes. *Women by Women: Five Contemporary English and French Canadian Novelists*. Diss. University of Connecticut, 1978.
Discusses *Le Temps sauvage*.

Rea, Annabelle. "The Climate of Viol/Violence and Madness in Anne Hébert's *Les Fous de Bassan*." *Québec Studies* 4 (1986): 170-83.
Discusses *In the Shadow of the Wind*.

Rose, Marilyn Gaddis. "When an Author Chooses French: Hébert and Chedid." *Québec Studies* 3 (1985): 148-59.
Discusses *Kamouraska*.

Rosenstreich, Susan L. "Counter-Traditions: The Marginal Poetics of Anne Hébert." *Traditionalism, Nationalism, and Feminism: Women Writers of Quebec*. Ed. Paula Gilbert Lewis. Westport, CT: Greenwood, 1985. 63-70.
Discusses *Poems* and *Les Songes en équilibre*.

Russell, D. W. "Anne Hébert: An Annotated Bibliography." *The Annotated Bibliography of Canada's Major Authors*. Ed. Robert Lecker and Jack David. 7 vols. to date. Toronto: ECW Press, 1979-. 7: 115-270.

Russell, Delbert W. *Anne Hébert*. Boston: Twayne, 1983.
Overview.

Russell, Delbert W. "Anne Hébert: 'Les Invités au procès.'" *Canadian Literature* 74 (1977): 30-39.
Discusses "The Guests on Trial."

Sachs, Murray. "Love on the Rocks: Anne Hébert's *Kamouraska*." *Traditionalism, Nationalism, and Feminism: Women Writers of Quebec*. Ed. Paula Gilbert Lewis. Westport, CT: Greenwood, 1985. 109-23.

Schub, Claire Elizabeth. *The Poetry of Anne Hébert: A Study of Poetic Consciousness*. Diss. Princeton University, 1986.
Overview of poetry.

Scott, Frank, and Anne Hébert. *Dialogue sur la traduction: à propos du* Tombeau des rois. Montreal: HMH, 1970.
Discusses *The Tomb of the Kings*.

Sénécal, André J. "*Les Fous de Bassan*: An Eschatology." *Québec Studies* 7 (1988): 150-60.
Discusses *In the Shadow of the Wind*.

Slott, Kathryn. "Repression, Obsession, and Re-Emergence in Hébert's *Les Fous de Bassan*." *American Review of Canadian Studies* 17.3 (1987): 297-307.
Discusses *In the Shadow of the Wind*.

Slott, Kathryn. "Submersion and Resugence of the Female Other in Anne Hébert's *Les Fous de Bassan*." *Québec Studies* 4 (1986): 158-69.
Discusses *In the Shadow of the Wind*.

Smith, Donald. "Anne Hébert and the Roots of Imagination." *Voices of Deliverance: Interviews with Quebec and Acadian Writers*. Trans. Larry Shouldice. Toronto: Anansi, 1986. 33-55.
Interview.

Stratford, Philip. "*Kamouraska* and *The Diviners*." *Review of National Literatures* 7 (1976): 110-26.

Stratford, Philip. "Territorial Prerogatives: Margaret Laurence and Anne Hébert." *All the Polarities: Comparative Studies in Contemporary Canadian Novels in French and English*. Toronto: ECW Press, 1986. 45-55.
Discusses *Kamouraska*.

Tomlinson, Muriel D. "A Comparison of *Les enfants terribles* and *Les chambres de bois.*" *Revue de l'Université d'Ottawa* 43.4 (1973): 532-39.
Discusses *The Silent Rooms.*

Tougas, Gérard. *History of French-Canadian Literature.* Trans. Alta Lind Cook. 2nd ed. Toronto: Ryerson Press, 1966. 176, 203-06.
Overview.

Urbas, Jeanette. "Society as Repression." *From* Thirty Acres *to Modern Times: The Story of French-Canadian Literature.* Toronto: McGraw-Hill Ryerson, 1976. 100-09.
Discusses *The Torrent*, *The Silent Rooms* and *Kamouraska.*

Waelti-Walters, Jennifer. "'Beauty and the Beast' and *The Silent Rooms* (Hébert)." *Fairy Tales and the Female Imagination.* Montreal: Eden, 1982. 13-30.

Weir, Lorraine. "Anne Hébert." *Canadian Writers, 1920-1959: First Series.* Ed. W. H. New. Dictionary of Literary Biography 68. Detroit: Gale, 1988. 166-74.
Overview.

Weir, Lorraine. "Fauna of Mirrors: The Poetry of Hébert and Atwood." *Ariel* 10.3 (1979): 99-113.
Discusses *The Tomb of the Kings.*

Wilson, Edmund. *O Canada: An American's Notes on Canadian Culture.* New York: Farrar, Straus and Giroux, 1964. 122, 123-27, 150.
Discusses *The Silent Rooms.*

Winspur, Steven. "Undoing the Novel of Authority with Anne Hébert." *Teaching Language Through Literature* 26.2 (1987): 24-32.
Discusses *In the Shadow of the Wind* and *The Tomb of the Kings.*

BOOK REVIEWS

ANNE HEBERT: SELECTED POEMS

Books in Canada Nov. 1980: 20.
University of Toronto Quarterly 50.4 (1981): 89-90.

CHILDREN OF THE BLACK SABBATH/LES ENFANTS DU SABBAT

Books in Canada Oct. 1977: 23-24.
Branching Out 4.4 (1977): 43-44.
Canadian Forum Aug. 1977: 39.
Canadian Literature 70 (1976): 79-81.
Essays on Canadian Writing 7-8 (1977): 31-35.
New York Times 7 Sept. 1977: C19.
New York Times Book Review 24 July 1977: 14-15.
Queen's Quarterly 85.3 (1978): 447-51.
Quill and Quire Apr. 1977: 38.
Times Literary Supplement 10 Oct. 1975: 1208.
University of Toronto Quarterly 47.4 (1978): 387-88.

DIALOGUE SUR LA TRADUCTION A PROPOS DU 'TOMBEAU DES ROIS'

French Review 45.1 (1971): 243-44.

HELOISE

Books in Canada Feb. 1983: 11-12.
Canadian Literature 91 (1981): 134-36.
Canadian Literature 117 (1988): 126-32.
Fiddlehead 141 (1984): 83-89.
French Review 54.5 (1981): 763-64.
Quill and Quire Jan. 1983: 30+.
University of Toronto Quarterly 52.4 (1983): 393-94.
West Coast Review 18.1 (1983): 60-64.

IN THE SHADOW OF THE WIND/LES FOUS DE BASSAN

Books in Canada Feb. 1984: 8+.
Canadian Book Review Annual (1983): 170.
Canadian Forum Mar. 1984: 37.
Canadian Literature 99 (1983): 132-34.
Canadian Literature 103 (1984): 129-31.
French Review 56.6 (1983): 978-79.
Maclean's 17 Oct. 1983: 61.
New Statesman 20 July 1984: 24.
New York Times Book Review 22 July 1984: 7.
Quill and Quire Nov. 1983: 20.
Saturday Night Feb. 1984: 66.
University of Toronto Quarterly 53.4 (1984): 406-07.
Women's Review of Books Nov. 1984: 15-16.
World Literature Today 57.3 (1983): 420.

KAMOURASKA

Antigonish Review 14 (1973): 111-13.
Books in Canada Apr.-June 1973: 1+.
Canadian Forum Nov.-Dec. 1973: 32-33.
English Quarterly 7.4 (1974-75): 89-92.
French Review 44.5 (1971): 961-62.
Open Letter 2nd ser.6 (1973): 121-23.
Queen's Quarterly 81.3 (1974): 474-76.
Quill and Quire June 1973: 13.
Saturday Night Aug. 1973: 32.
Times Literary Supplement 2 Apr. 1971: 402.
University of Toronto Quarterly 43.4 (1974): 343.

POEMS/POEMES

Books in Canada Dec. 1975: 24.
Brick 2 (1978): 52-54.
Canadian Book Review Annual (1975): 143.
Canadian Forum Aug. 1976: 38-39.
Canadian Literature 71 (1976): 87-89.
Contemporary Verse 2 2.1 (1976): 18-20.
Essays on Canadian Writing 7-8 (1977): 31-35.
Matrix 2.1 (1976): 22-23.
Meta 21.2 (1976): 165-68.
Queen's Quarterly 85.1 (1978): 151-52.
Quill and Quire Nov. 1975: 31.
Waves 4.2 (1976): 13-16.

LE PREMIER JARDIN

Books in Canada June-July 1988: 23-24.

THE SILENT ROOMS/LES CHAMBRES DE BOIS

Books in Canada Feb. 1975: 19.
Canadian Fiction Magazine 19 (1975): 95-102.
Canadian Literature 65 (1975): 117-18.
Journal of Canadian Fiction 4.3 (1975): 173-75.
Maclean's Jan. 1975: 71.
Quill and Quire Dec. 1974: 22-23.
Room of One's Own 1.2 (1975): 75-76.
University of Toronto Quarterly 44.4 (1975): 310.
University of Windsor Review 10.2 (1975): 82-87.

LES SONGES EN EQUILIBRE

University of Toronto Quarterly 12.3 (1943): 342-44.

ST-DENYS GARNEAU AND ANNE HEBERT

British Columbia Library Quarterly 26.3: 29+.
Canadian Forum Dec. 1962: 210.
Queen's Quarterly 70.3 (1963): 449-50.
Tamarack Review 29 (1963): 80-82.

THE TOMB OF THE KINGS/LE TOMBEAU DES ROIS

Culture 29 (1968): 254-59.
Poetry 112.3 (1968): 201-05.
University of Toronto Quarterly 23.3 (1954): 325-26.

THE TORRENT/LE TORRENT

Canadian Fiction Magazine 15 (1974): 97-99.
Chelsea Journal Mar.-Apr. 1979: 79.
Journal of Canadian Fiction 3.2 (1974): 105-06.
Journal of Commonwealth Literature 11.3 (1977): 82.
Saturday Night Feb. 1974: 34-35.
University of Toronto Quarterly 20.4 (1951): 397-98.

HEMON, LOUIS (1880-1913)

WORKS BY LOUIS HEMON

Maria Chapdelaine. Montreal: J. A. Le Febvre, 1916. *Maria Chapdelaine: A Tale of the Lake St. John Country*. Trans. W. H. Blake. Toronto: Macmillan, 1921. *Maria Chapdelaine*. Trans. Sir Andrew MacPhail. Montreal: A. T. Chapman, 1921.

La Belle que voilà. Paris: B. Grasset, 1923. *My Fair Lady*. Trans. William Aspenwall Bradley. New York: Macmillan, 1923.

Collin-Maillard. Paris: Grasset, 1924. *Blind Man's Buff*. Trans. Arthur Richmond. London: Macmillan, 1924.

The Journal of Louis Hémon. Trans. William Aspenwall Bradley. New York: Macmillan, 1924.

Battling Malone, pugiliste. Paris: Grasset, 1925. *Battling Malone and Other Stories*. Trans. William Aspenwall Bradley. London: T. Butterworth, 1925.

Itinéraire. Paris: B. Grasset, 1927.

Monsieur Ripois et la Némésis. Paris: Grasset, 1950. *Monsieur Ripois and Nemesis*. Trans. William Aspenwall Bradley. New York: Macmillan, 1925.

Lettres à sa famille. Ed. Nicole Deschamps. Montreal: Presses de l'Université de Montréal, 1968.

WORKS ABOUT LOUIS HEMON

Atwood, Margaret. *Survival: A Thematic Guide to Canadian Literature*. Toronto: Anansi, 1972. 136, 218-19. Discusses *Maria Chapdelaine*.

Blake, W. H., trans. Introduction. *Maria Chapdelaine*. By Louis Hémon. Laurentian Library 17. Toronto: Macmillan, 1973. v-xiii.

Boyd, Ernest. "Canadian-French Fiction." *Studies From Ten Literatures*. Port Washington, NY: Kennikat Press, 1968. 297-303.
Discusses *Maria Chapdelaine*.

Call, Frank Oliver. "Country of *Maria Chapdelaine*." *Canadian Magazine* Dec. 1924: 453-61.
General.

Cogswell, Fred. "The French-Canadian Novel and the Problem of Social Change." *Journal of Canadian Fiction* 1.2 (1972): 65-68.
Discusses *Maria Chapdelaine*.

Coulon, Jacques L. "Sur les pas de Louis Hémon, au pays de *Maria Chapdelaine*; The Footsteps of Louis Hémon in the Country of *Maria Chapdelaine*." Trans. Sylvia Sealey. *Canadian Geographical Journal* 63.5 (1961): 184-91.
General.

Dorsinville, Max. *Caliban Without Prospero: Essay on Quebec and Black Literature*. Erin, Ont.: Porcépic, 1974. 59-75.
Discusses *Maria Chapdelaine*.

Eayrs, Hugh. Introduction. *Maria Chapdelaine*. By Louis Hémon. Trans. W. H. Blake. Toronto: Macmillan, 1938. n. pag.

Fitzpatrick, Marjorie A. "Teaching French-Canadian Civilization Through the Literature: Hémon, Roy, and Blais." *Québec Studies* 2 (1984): 82-93.
Discusses *Maria Chapdelaine*.

Grove, F. P. "Peasant Poetry and Fiction from Hesiod to Hémon." *Royal Society of Canada. Transactions* 3rd ser. 38 sect. 2 (1944): 89-98.
Discusses *Maria Chapdelaine*.

Hicks, R. K. "French Canada in Fiction." *Dalhousie Review* 2 (1922): 216-29.
Discusses *Maria Chapdelaine*.

Lennox, John. "*La Scouine*: Influences and Significance." *Studies in Canadian Literature* 5 (1980): 47-62.
Discusses *Maria Chapdelaine*.

McAndrew, Allan. "*Maria Chapdelaine* Chez Elle." *University of Toronto Quarterly* 15.1 (1945): 76-85.

McNaught, Carlton. "The Real *Maria Chapdelaine*." *Canadian Magazine* Jan. 1935: 6+.

O'Neill-Karch, Mariel. "Louis Hémon." *Profiles in Canadian Literature*. Ed. Jeffrey M. Heath. Toronto: Dundurn Press, 1982. 3: 57-64.
Discusses *Maria Chapdelaine*.

Osborne, W. F. "The Qualities of *Maria Chapdelaine*." *Queen's Quarterly* 46.4 (1939): 461-67.

"Peribonca Bella." *Time* (*Can. ed.*) 29 Nov. 1948: 24.
Discusses *Maria Chapdelaine*.

Sandwell, B. K. "Maria's Revenge." *Saturday Night* 18 June 1938: 12.
Discusses *Maria Chapdelaine*.

Sandwell, B. K. "Topics of the Day." *Canadian Home Journal* Aug. 1938: 23.
Discusses *Maria Chapdelaine*.

Sutherland, Ronald. *Second Image: Comparative Studies in Quebec/Canadian Literature*. Toronto: New Press, 1971. 4-6.
Discusses *Maria Chapdelaine*.

Sutherland, Ronald. "Twin Solitudes." *Canadian Literature* 31 (1967): 5-24.
Discusses *Maria Chapdelaine*.

Tougas, Gérard. *History of French-Canadian Literature*. Trans. Alta Lind Cook. 2nd ed. Toronto: Ryerson Press, 1966. 112-15.
Discusses *Maria Chapdelaine*.

Truffaut, François. "René Clément: Monsieur Ripois." *The Films in My Life*. Trans. Leonard Mayhew. New York: Simon and Schuster, 1978. 197-200.
Discusses *Monsieur Ripois and Nemesis*.

Urbas, Jeanette. "The Myth of the Land." *From* Thirty Acres *to Modern Times: The Story of French-Canadian Literature*. Toronto: McGraw-Hill Ryerson, 1976. 9-18.
Discusses *Maria Chapdelaine*.

van Lent, Peter. "Absence and Departure: The Male Mystique in French-Canadian Literature Before 1950." *American Review of Canadian Studies* 16.1 (1986): 17-23.
Discusses *Maria Chapdelaine.*

van Lent, Peter. "*Maria Chapdelaine*: A Controversial Text." *Québec Studies* 1.1 (1983): 224-31.

Whiteman, Bruce. "The Publication of *Maria Chapdelaine* in English." *Papers of the Bibliographical Society of Canada/Cahiers de la Société bibliographique du Canada* 21 (1982): 52-59.

Wilson, Edmund. *O Canada: An American's Notes on Canadian Culture.* New York: Farrar, Straus and Giroux, 1964. 140-45.
Discusses *Maria Chapdelaine.*

"'With Tender Eyes.'" *Saturday Night* 10 Jan. 1950: 11.
Discusses *Maria Chapdelaine.*

Zieman, Margaret-K. "Louis Hémon: Vagabond Genius." *Maclean's Magazine* 15 June 1953: 20-21+.
Discusses *Maria Chapdelaine.*

Zieman, Margaret K. "Origins of *Maria Chapdelaine.*" *Canadian Literature* 20 (1964): 41-53.

BOOK REVIEWS

BATTLING MALONE AND OTHER STORIES/BATTLING MALONE, PUGILISTE

Times Literary Supplement 22 Oct. 1925: 694.

BLIND MAN'S BUFF/COLLIN-MAILLARD

Dial Sept. 1925: 259.
London Mercury Feb. 1925: 429-31.
New Republic 15 Oct. 1924: 183-84.
New York Times Book Review 30 Mar. 1924: 8.
New York Times Book Review 8 Feb. 1925: 9.
Saturday Review of Literature 28 Mar. 1925: 627.
Times Literary Supplement 13 Mar. 1924: 156.
Times Literary Supplement 11 Dec. 1924: 846.

ITINERAIRE

University of Toronto Quarterly 57.1 (1987): 179-82.

THE JOURNAL OF LOUIS HEMON

New York Times Book Review 4 Jan. 1925: 12.

MARIA CHAPDELAINE

Canadian Forum Dec. 1921: 470+.
Canadian Forum Feb. 1935: 201.
Dublin Review 171 (1922): 124-30.
Modern Language Journal 8 (1924): 313-17.
Nation 1 Feb. 1922: 126.
New York Times Book Review 25 Dec. 1921: 24.
Yale Review ns 11 (1922): 860-64.

MONSIEUR RIPOIS AND NEMESIS/MONSIEUR RIPOIS ET LA NEMESIS

Canadian Forum Mar. 1926: 190-91.
New Republic 19 Aug. 1925: 351-52.
New Statesman 18 July 1925: 396.
New York Times Book Review 5 Apr. 1925: 8.
Saturday Review of Literature 27 June 1925: 851-52.
Times Literary Supplement 28 May 1925: 366.

MY FAIR LADY/LA BELLE QUE VOILA

Nation 2 Apr. 1924: 375-76.
New Republic 15 Oct. 1924: 183-84.
New York Times Book Review 3 June 1923: 7.
New York Times Book Review 9 Dec. 1923: 9.
Times Literary Supplement 19 Apr. 1923: 263.

JASMIN, CLAUDE (1930-)

WORKS BY CLAUDE JASMIN

La Corde au cou. Montreal: Cercle du Livre de France, 1960.

Délivrez-nous du mal. Montreal: Editions à la Page, 1961; rev. Montreal: Editions Internationales Stanké, 1980.

Blues pour un homme averti. Ottawa: Parti Pris, 1964.

Ethel et le terroriste. Montreal: Déom, 1964. *Ethel and the Terrorist*. Trans. David S. Walker. Montreal: Harvest House, 1965.

Et puis tout est silence. Montreal: Editions de l'Homme, 1965. *The Rest is Silence*. Trans. David Lobdell. Ottawa: Oberon, 1981.

Pleure pas, Germaine. Montreal: Parti Pris, 1965.

Roussil manifeste. Montreal: Editions du Jour, 1965.

Les Artisans créateurs. Montreal: Lidec, 1967.

Les Coeurs empaillés. Montreal: Parti Pris, 1967.

Rimbaud, mon beau salaud! Montreal: Editions du Jour, 1969.

Jasmin: dossier sur moi même. Montreal: Claude Langevin, 1970.

Tuez le veau gras. Montreal: Leméac, 1970.

L'Outaragasipi. Montreal: L'Actuelle, 1971.

C'est toujours la même histoire. Montreal: Leméac, 1972.

La Petite Patrie. Montreal: La Presse, 1972.

Pointe-Calumet boogie-woogie. Montreal: La Presse, 1973.

Sainte-Adèle-la-Vaisselle. Montreal: La Presse, 1974.

Danielle, ça va marcher! Montreal: Stanké, 1975.

Feu à volonté. Montreal: Leméac, 1976.

Le Loup de Brunswick City. Montreal: Leméac, 1976.

Revoir Ethel. Montreal: Stanké, 1976.

Feu sur la télévision. Montreal: Leméac, 1977.

La Sablière. Montreal: Leméac, 1979. *Mario*. Trans. David Lobdell. Ottawa: Oberon, 1985.

Le Veau dort. Montreal: Leméac, 1979.

Les Contes du Sommet-bleu. Montreal: Québécor, 1980. *The Dragon and Other Laurentian Tales*. Trans. Pat Sillers. Toronto: Oxford, 1987.

L'Armoire de Pantagruel. Montreal: Leméac, 1982.

Maman-Paris, Maman-la-France. Montreal: Leméac, 1982.

Deux mâts, une galère. With Edouard Jasmin. Montreal: Leméac, 1983.

Le Crucifié du Sommet-Bleu. Montreal: Leméac, 1984.

L'Etat-macquereau, l'état maffia. Montreal: Leméac, 1984.

Des Cons qui s'adorent. Montreal: Leméac, 1985.

Une Duchesse à Ogunquit. Montreal: Leméac, 1985.

Alice vous fait dire bon soir. Montreal: Leméac, 1986.

Safari au centre-ville. Montreal: Leméac, 1987.

Une Saison en studio. Montreal: Guérin, 1987.

Pour tout vous dire. Montreal: Guérin, 1988.

WORKS ABOUT CLAUDE JASMIN

Bond, David J. "Claude Jasmin's Fictional World." *International Fiction Review* 3.2 (1976): 113-19.
Overview.

Brazeau, J. Raymond. "Claude Jasmin." *An Outline of Contemporary French Canadian Literature.* Toronto: Forum House, 1972. 83-98.
Overview.

Falardeau, Jean Charles. "The Evolution of the Hero in the Quebec Novel." *Contemporary Quebec Criticism.* Ed. and trans. Larry Shouldice. Toronto: University of Toronto Press, 1979. 95-116.
Overview.

Mitcham, Allison. "Imagination and the Capacity to Dream: A Study in Contemporary Canadian Fiction." *Revue de l'Université de Moncton* 6.3 (1973): 75-80.
Discusses *Ethel and the Terrorist.*

Raoul, Valerie. "Claude Jasmin." *Canadian Writers Since 1960: Second Series.* Ed. W. H. New. Dictionary of Literary Biography 60. Detroit: Gale, 1987. 139-45.
Overview.

Shek, Ben-Zion. "The Jew in the French-Canadian Novel." *Viewpoints* 4.4 (1969): 29-35.
Discusses *Ethel and the Terrorist* and *La Corde au cou.*

Shek, Ben-Zion. *Social Realism in the French-Canadian Novel.* Montreal: Harvest House, 1977. 245-57.
Discusses *La Corde au cou* and *Ethel and the Terrorist.*

Sutherland, Ronald. "The Fourth Separatism." *Canadian Literature* 45 (1970): 7-23.
Discusses *Ethel and the Terrorist.*

Urbas, Jeanette. "From Individual Revolt to Social Revolution." *From* Thirty Acres *to Modern Times: The Story of French-Canadian Literature.* Toronto: McGraw-Hill Ryerson, 1976. 141-46.
Discusses *Ethel and the Terrorist.*

BOOK REVIEWS

DEUX MATS, UNE GALERE

Canadian Literature 103 (1984): 81-83.

THE DRAGON AND OTHER LAURENTIAN TALES/LES CONTES DU SOMMET-BLEU

Canadian Literature 117 (1988): 151-54.
University of Toronto Quarterly 58.1 (1988): 83-84.

ETHEL AND THE TERRORIST/ETHEL ET LE TERRORISTE

Canadian Literature 67 (1976): 109-12.
Chelsea Journal Mar.-Apr. 1979: 78-79.
Journal of Canadian Fiction 19 (1977): 134-37.

MARIO/LA SABLIERE

Books in Canada Jan.-Feb. 1986: 23.
Canadian Book Review Annual (1985): 149.
Canadian Literature 88 (1981): 93-96.
Canadian Literature 112 (1987): 104-07.
Queen's Quarterly 94.2 (1987): 366-75.
University of Toronto Quarterly 56.1 (1986): 73.
World Literature Today 54.4 (1980): 595-96.

PLEURE PAS, GERMAINE

French Review 49.2 (1975): 299.

THE REST IS SILENCE/ET PUIS TOUT EST SILENCE

Books in Canada Dec. 1981: 27-28.
Canadian Book Review Annual (1981): 138.
Canadian Literature 55 (1973): 114-15.

REVOIR ETHEL

Fiddlehead 112 (1977): 161-64.
Tamarack Review 71 (1977): 82-90.

LABERGE, ALBERT (1871-1960)

WORKS BY ALBERT LABERGE

La Scouine. Montreal: Imprimerie Modèle, 1918. *Bitter Bread*. Trans. Conrad Dion. Montreal: Harvest House, 1977.

Quand chantait la cigale. Montreal: n.p., 1936.

Visages de la vie et de la mort. Montreal: n.p., 1936.

Peintres et écrivains d'hier et d'aujourd'hui. Montreal: n.p., 1938.

La Fin du voyage. Montreal: n.p., 1942.

Scènes de chaque jour. Montreal: n.p., 1942.

Journalistes, écrivains et artistes. Montreal: n.p., 1945.

Charles de Belle, peintre-poète. Montreal: n.p., 1949.

Le Destin des hommes. Montreal: n.p., 1950.

Fin du roman. Montreal: n.p., 1951.

Images de la vie. Montreal: n.p., 1952.

Le Dernier Souper. Montreal: n.p., 1953.

Propos sur nos écrivains. Montreal: n.p., 1954.

Hymnes à la terre. Montreal: n.p., 1955.

Anthologie d'Albert Laberge. Ed. Gérard Bessette. Montreal: Cercle du Livre de France, 1963.

WORKS ABOUT ALBERT LABERGE

Cagnon, Maurice. *The French Novel of Quebec*. Boston: Twayne, 1986. 21-23.
Discusses *Bitter Bread*.

Dion, Conrad, trans. "Albert Laberge." *Bitter Bread.* By Albert Laberge. Montreal: Harvest House, 1977. n. pag.

Lennox, John. "*La Scouine*: Influences and Significance." *Studies in Canadian Literature* 5 (1980): 47-62.
Discusses *Bitter Bread.*

Shek, B.-Z. "Albert Laberge." *Canadian Writers, 1920-1959: First Series.* Ed. W. H. New. Dictionary of Literary Biography 68. Detroit: Gale, 1988. 211-13.
Overview.

Shek, Ben-Zion. *Social Realism in the French-Canadian Novel.* Montreal: Harvest House, 1977. 52-54.
Discusses *Bitter Bread.*

Tougas, Gérard. *History of French-Canadian Literature.* Trans. Alta Lind Cook. 2nd ed. Toronto: Ryerson Press, 1966. 122-26.
Discusses *Bitter Bread.*

BOOK REVIEWS

BITTER BREAD/LA SCOUINE

Books in Canada Mar. 1978: 33.
Canadian Book Review Annual (1977): 110-11.
Canadian Literature 82 (1979): 120-22.
Quill and Quire Jan. 1978: 26-27.
University of Toronto Quarterly 47.4 (1978): 390-91.
University of Toronto Quarterly 58.1 (1988): 185-88.

LANGEVIN, ANDRE (1927-)

WORKS BY ANDRE LANGEVIN

Evadé de la nuit. Montreal: Cercle du Livre de France, 1951.

Poussière sur la ville. Montreal: Cercle du Livre de France, 1953. *Dust Over the City*. Trans. John Latrobe and Robert Gottlieb. Toronto: McClelland and Stewart, 1955.

Le Temps des hommes. Montreal: Cercle du Livre de France, 1956.

L'Oeil du peuple. Montreal: Cercle du Livre de France, 1958.

L'Elan d'Amérique. Montreal: Cercle du Livre de France, 1972.

Une Chaîne dans le parc. Montreal: Cercle du Livre de France, 1974. *Orphan Street*. Trans. Alan Brown. Toronto: McClelland and Stewart, 1976.

WORKS ABOUT ANDRE LANGEVIN

Bessette, Gérard. "French-Canadian Society as Seen by Contemporary Novelists." *Queen's Quarterly* 69.2 (1962): 177-97.
Discusses *Dust Over the City* and *Le Temps des hommes.*

Bond, David J. *The Temptation of Despair: A Study of the Quebec Novelist André Langevin*. Fredericton, N.B.: York Press, 1982.
Overview.

Cagnon, Maurice. *The French Novel of Quebec*. Boston: Twayne, 1986. 51-55.
Discusses *Evadé de la nuit*, *Dust Over the City* and *Le Temps des hommes.*

Collin, W. E. "André Langevin and the Problem of Suffering." *Tamarack Review* 10 (1959): 77-92.
Overview.

Falardeau, Jean Charles. "The Evolution of the Hero in the Quebec Novel." *Contemporary Quebec Criticism*. Ed. and trans. Larry Shouldice. Toronto: University of Toronto Press, 1979. 95-116.
Discusses *Evadé de la nuit*, *Dust Over the City* and *Le Temps des hommes*.

Harger-Grinling, V. A. "André Langevin." *Canadian Writers Since 1960: Second Series*. Ed. W. H. New. Dictionary of Literary Biography 60. Detroit: Gale, 1987. 168-71.
Overview.

Hodgson, Richard G. "Time and Space in André Langevin's *L'Elan d'Amérique*." *Canadian Literature* 88 (1981): 31-38.

May, Cedric. *Breaking the Silence: The Literature of Québec*. Birmingham, Eng.: University of Birmingham, Regional Studies Centre, 1981. 94-97.
Discusses *Dust Over the City*.

Mitcham, Allison. "Flight: A Comparative Ecological Study Based on Contemporary French and English-Canadian Fiction." *Revue de l'Université de Moncton* 6.2 (1973): 86-105.
Discusses *Le Temps des hommes* and *Evadé de la nuit*.

Mitcham, Allison. *The Northern Imagination: A Study of Northern Canadian Literature*. Moonbeam, Ont.: Penumbra, 1983. passim.
Overview.

Purdy, Anthony. "Stopping the Kaleidoscope: The Logic of Life and the Logic of Story in André Langevin's *Poussière sur la ville*." *Dalhousie French Studies* 8 (1985): 78-102.
Discusses *Dust Over the City*.

Socken, Paul. "Alain Dubois's Commitment: A Reading of *Poussière sur la ville*." *International Fiction Review* 4.2 (1977): 174-77.
Discusses *Dust Over the City*.

Stratford, Philip. "The Two Sides of Main Street: Sinclair Ross and André Langevin." *All the Polarities: Comparative Studies in Contemporary Canadian Novels in French and English*. Toronto: ECW Press, 1986. 30-44.
Discusses *Dust Over the City*.

Sutherland, Ronald. Introduction. *Dust Over the City*. By André Langevin. Trans. John Latrobe and Robert Gottlieb. New Canadian Library 113. Toronto: McClelland and Stewart, 1974. n. pag.

Sutherland, Ronald. *The New Hero: Essays in Comparative Quebec/Canadian Literature*. Toronto: Macmillan, 1977. 13-16, 51-57.
Discusses *Orphan Street* and *Dust Over the City*.

Tougas, Gérard. *History of French-Canadian Literature*. Trans. Alta Lind Cook. 2nd ed. Toronto: Ryerson Press, 1966. 160-63.
Overview.

Urbas, Jeanette. "The Search for Meaning." *From* Thirty Acres *to Modern Times: The Story of French-Canadian Literature*. Toronto: McGraw-Hill Ryerson, 1976. 70-75.
Discusses *Dust Over the City*.

Warwick, Jack. *The Long Journey: Literary Themes of French Canada*. Toronto: University of Toronto Press, 1968. 124-27, 144-59.
Discusses *Dust Over the City* and *Le Temps des hommes*.

Wilson, Edmund. *O Canada: An American's Notes on Canadian Culture*. New York: Farrar, Straus and Giroux, 1964. 167-72.
Discusses *Dust Over the City*, *Le Temps des hommes* and *Evadé de la nuit*.

BOOK REVIEWS

DUST OVER THE CITY/POUSSIERE SUR LA VILLE

Canadian Fiction Magazine 32-33 (1979-80): 172-77.
Journal of Canadian Fiction 3.4 (1975): 87-89.
New York Times Book Review 18 Sept. 1955: 31.
Queen's Quarterly 63.1 (1956): 126-30.
Saturday Review of Literature 17 Sept. 1955: 28.
University of Toronto Quarterly 23.3 (1954): 315-17.

L'ELAN D'AMERIQUE

Canadian Fiction Magazine 32-33 (1979-80): 172-77.

EVADE DE LA NUIT

University of Toronto Quarterly 21.4 (1952): 396-98.

ORPHAN STREET/UNE CHAINE DANS LE PARC

Canadian Fiction Magazine 32-33 (1979-80): 172-77.
Dalhousie Review 57.1 (1977): 162-65.
Queen's Quarterly 84.3 (1977): 510-12.
Quill and Quire Nov. 1976: 33.
Saturday Night Nov. 1976: 56-58.

LE TEMPS DES HOMMES

University of Toronto Quarterly 26.3 (1957): 388-89.

LEMELIN, ROGER (1919-)

WORKS BY ROGER LEMELIN

Au pied de la pente douce. Montreal: L'Arbre, 1944. *The Town Below*. Trans. Samuel Putnam. New York: Reynal and Hitchcock, 1948.

Les Plouffe. Quebec: Bélisle, 1948. *The Plouffe Family*. Trans. Mary Finch. Toronto: McClelland and Stewart, 1950.

Fantaisies sur les péchés capitaux. Montreal: Beauchemin, 1949.

Pierre le magnifique. Quebec: Institut littéraire du Québec, 1952. *In Quest of Splendour*. Trans. Harry Lorin Binsse. Toronto: McClelland and Stewart, 1955.

L'Ecrivain et le Journaliste. Montreal: La Presse, 1977.

Langue, Esthétique et Morale. Montreal: La Presse, 1977.

L'Unité canadienne et la liberté. [s.l.]: [s.n.], 1979. *Canadian Unity and Freedom*. Montreal: La Presse, 1979.

Les Voies de l'espérance. Montreal: La Presse, 1979.

La Culotte en or. Montreal: La Presse, 1980.

Le Crime d'Ovide Plouffe. Quebec: ETR, 1982. *The Crime of Ovide Plouffe*. Trans. Alan Brown. Toronto: McClelland and Stewart, 1984.

WORKS ABOUT ROGER LEMELIN

Atwood, Margaret. *Survival: A Thematic Guide to Canadian Literature*. Toronto: Anansi, 1972. 132-33.
Discusses "The Legacy" in *Canadian Short Stories*, ed. Robert Weaver.

Binsse, Harry Lorin, trans. Preface. *In Quest of Splendour*. By Roger Lemelin. Toronto: McClelland and Stewart, 1955. 7-10.

Cagnon, Maurice. *The French Novel of Quebec*. Boston: Twayne, 1986. 29-31.
Discusses *The Town Below* and *The Plouffe Family*.

Charney, Ann. "Family Reunion: In the 1950's the Plouffes Were Canada's Most Popular Television Family." *Today* 25 Apr. 1981: 12-14.
Discusses *The Plouffe Family*.

Collin, W. E. "Roger Lemelin: The Pursuit of Grandeur." *Queen's Quarterly* 61.2 (1954): 195-212.
Discusses *The Plouffe Family*, *In Quest of Splendour* and *The Town Below*.

Dorsinville, Max. *Caliban Without Prospero: Essay on Quebec and Black Literature*. Erin, Ont.: Porcépic, 1974. 105-33.
Discusses *The Town Below*.

Keate, Stuart. "The Boy from the Town Below." *Maclean's Magazine* 1 Feb. 1950: 17+.
General.

"Lemelin Papers to National Library." *Quill and Quire* Nov. 1982: 21.
General.

Lemelin, Roger. "I Stole Only for the Good of the Family." *Today* 8 May 1982: 5.
Autobiographical.

Lemelin, Roger. "My First Novel." *Queen's Quarterly* 61.2 (1954): 189-94.
Autobiographical.

Lemelin, Roger. "Quebec, I Love You. Quebec City Serves as the Main Backdrop for the Works of Novelist and Scriptwriter Roger Lemelin." *Forces* 82 (1988): 13-15.
General.

Lennox, John. "*La Scouine*: Influences and Significance." *Studies in Canadian Literature* 5 (1980): 47-62.
Discusses *The Town Below*.

Moss, John. Introduction. *The Plouffe Family*. By Roger Lemelin. Trans. Mary Finch. New Canadian Library 119. Toronto: McClelland and Stewart, 1975. v-xiii.

"Native Product." *Time* (*Can. ed.*) 1 Nov. 1948: 24.
Discusses *The Plouffe Family*.

Parris, David L. "Cats in the Literature of Quebec." *British Journal of Canadian Studies* 3.2 (1988): 259-66.
Discusses *The Plouffe Family*.

Posner, Michael. "Seekers and Finders: Roger Lemelin: Making Success Sound Simple." *Impetus* Oct. 1974: 6-7+.
Biographical.

Putnam, Samuel, trans. Introductory Note. *The Town Below*. By Roger Lemelin. New York: Reynal and Hitchcock, 1948. xi-xiii.

Rodger, Ian. "No Time for Discussing the Sex of Angels." *Financial Post* 1 July 1972: 6.
General.

Sandwell, B. K. "*Plouffe Family* Is a Great Study in Nationalism of Quebec." *Saturday Night* 1 Feb. 1949: 7.

Shek, Ben-Zion. "The Jew in the French Canadian Novel." *Viewpoints* 4.4 (1969): 29-35.
Discusses *The Plouffe Family*.

Shek, Ben-Zion. "The World of Roger Lemelin." *Social Realism in the French-Canadian Novel*. Montreal: Harvest House, 1977. 112-56.
Discusses *The Town Below*, *The Plouffe Family* and *In Quest of Splendour*.

Shortliffe, Glen. Introduction. *The Town Below*. By Roger Lemelin. Trans. Samuel Putnam. New Canadian Library 26. Toronto: McClelland and Stewart, 1961. v-ix.

Thomas, David. "Roger Lemelin: The Cap Rouge Gadfly." *Maclean's* 18 June 1979: 4+.
General.

Tougas, Gérard. *History of French-Canadian Literature*. Trans. Alta Lind Cook. 2nd ed. Toronto: Ryerson Press, 1966. 158-60.
Overview.

Urbas, Jeanette. "Defeated Aspirations." *From* Thirty Acres *to Modern Times: The Story of French-Canadian Literature.* Toronto: McGraw-Hill Ryerson, 1976. 35-44.
Discusses *The Town Below, The Plouffe Family* and *In Quest of Splendour.*

Warwick, Jack. *The Long Journey: Literary Themes of French Canada.* Toronto: University of Toronto Press, 1968. 118-19.
Discusses *In Quest of Splendour.*

Wilson, Edmund. *O Canada: An American's Notes on Canadian Culture.* New York: Farrar, Straus and Giroux, 1964. 157-67.
Discusses *The Town Below, The Plouffe Family* and *In Quest of Splendour.*

BOOK REVIEWS

THE CRIME OF OVIDE PLOUFFE/LE CRIME D'OVIDE PLOUFFE

Books in Canada Apr. 1985: 26-27.
Canadian Book Review Annual (1984): 194.
Canadian Literature 109 (1986): 115-17.
University of Toronto Quarterly 54.4 (1985): 391-92.

LES FANTAISIES SUR LES PECHES CAPITAUX

University of Toronto Quarterly 19.4 (1950): 403-04.

IN QUEST OF SPLENDOUR/PIERRE LE MAGNIFIQUE

Canadian Forum Apr. 1956: 20.
Queen's Quarterly 63.1 (1956): 126-30.
Times Literary Supplement 2 Mar. 1956: 129.
University of Toronto Quarterly 22.4 (1953): 398-400.

THE PLOUFFE FAMILY/LES PLOUFFE

Canadian Book Review Annual (1975): 114-15.
Canadian Forum Mar. 1951: 287.
Times Literary Supplement 6 June 1952: 373.
University of Toronto Quarterly 18.4 (1949): 373-74.

THE TOWN BELOW/AU PIED DE LA PENTE DOUCE

Canadian Forum Sept. 1948: 143.
Commonweal 10 Sept. 1948: 527-28.
New York Times Book Review 18 Apr. 1948: 7.
New Yorker 24 Apr. 1948: 104.
Saturday Night 8 May 1948: 29.
Saturday Review of Literature 22 May 1948: 19+.
Time (*Can. ed.*) 10 May 1948: 64.
University of Toronto Quarterly 14.3 (1945): 283-84.

MAHEUX-FORCIER, LOUISE (1929-)

WORKS BY LOUISE MAHEUX-FORCIER

Amadou. Montreal: Cercle du Livre de France, 1963. *Amadou*. Trans. David Lobdell. Ottawa: Oberon, 1987.

L'île joyeuse. Montreal: Cercle du Livre de France, 1964. *Isle of Joy*. Trans. David Lobdell. Ottawa: Oberon, 1987.

Une Forêt pour Zoé. Montreal: Cercle du Livre de France, 1969. *A Forest for Zoe*. Trans. David Lobdell. Ottawa: Oberon, 1986.

Paroles et musiques. Montreal: Cercle du Livre de France, 1973.

Neige et palmiers, suivi de Le Violencelle. Montreal: Cercle du Livre de France, 1974.

Un Arbre chargé d'oiseaux: téléthéâtre, précédé de Journal de la maison d'Irène. Ottawa: Editions de l'Université d'Ottawa, 1976.

Le Coeur étoilé: suivi de Chrysanthème et de Miroir de nuit. Montreal: Pierre Tisseyre, 1977.

Appassionata. Montreal: Cercle du Livre de France, 1978.

En toutes lettres. Montreal: Pierre Tisseyre, 1980. *Letter by Letter*. Trans. David Lobdell. Ottawa: Oberon, 1982.

Arioso, suivi de Le Papier d'Arménie. Montreal: Pierre Tisseyre, 1981.

Un Parc en automne. Montreal: Pierre Tisseyre, 1982.

Le Sablier: journal intime 1981-1984. Montreal: Pierre Tisseyre, 1984.

Le Piano rouge, suivi de Comme un oiseau. Montreal: Cercle du Livre de France, 1985.

Un Jardin défendu, suivi de A la Brunante. Montreal: Pierre Tisseyre, 1988.

WORKS ABOUT LOUISE MAHEUX-FORCIER

Cagnon, Maurice. *The French Novel of Quebec.* Boston: Twayne, 1986. 90-97.
Discusses *Amadou, Isle of joy* and *A Forest for Zoe.*

Cagnon, Maurice. "Louise Maheux-Forcier and the Poetics of Sensuality." *Québec Studies* 1.1 (1983): 286-97. Rpt. in *Traditionalism, Nationalism, and Feminism: Women Writers of Quebec.* Ed. Paula Gilbert Lewis. Westport, CT: Greenwood, 1985. 95-107.
Discusses *Amadou* and *A Forest for Zoe.*

Dufault, Roseanna. "Personal and Political Childhood in Quebec: Analogies for Identity." *Continental, Latin-American and Francophone Women Writers.* Ed. Eunice Myers and Ginette Adamson. Lanham, MD: UP of America, 1987. 63-69.
Discusses *Isle of Joy.*

Raoul, Valerie. "Louise Maheux-Forcier." *Canadian Writers Since 1960: Second Series.* Ed. W. H. New. Dictionary of Literary Biography 60. Detroit: Gale 1987. 188-91.
Overview.

BOOK REVIEWS

AMADOU

Books in Canada Apr. 1988: 26-27.
Fiddlehead 156 (1988): 103-07.
University of Toronto Quarterly 58.1 (1988): 93.

UN ARBRE CHARGE D'OISEAUX

French Review 51.6 (1978): 916-17.

ARIOSO SUIVI DE LE PAPIER D'ARMENIE

French Review 56.4 (1983): 668-69.

A FOREST FOR ZOE/UNE FORET POUR ZOE

Books in Canada June-July 1987: 17-18.
Canadian Book Review Annual (1987): 131.
Canadian Literature 115 (1987): 208-09.
Cross-Canada Writers' Quarterly 9.3-4 (1987): 48-49.

ISLE OF JOY/L'ILE JOYEUSE

Books in Canada Apr. 1988: 26-27.
Fiddlehead 156 (1988): 103-07.
University of Toronto Quarterly 58.1 (1988): 93.

LETTER BY LETTER/EN TOUTES LETTRES

Canadian Book Review Annual (1982): 210.
French Review 55.2 (1981): 306.
Quarry 33.3 (1984): 88-91.
Quill and Quire Apr. 1983: 22.
University of Toronto Quarterly 52.4 (1983): 392.

UN PARC EN AUTOMNE

Canadian Literature 102 (1984): 98-101.

MAILLET, ANTONINE (1929-)

WORKS BY ANTONINE MAILLET

Pointe-aux-coques. Montreal: Fides, 1958.

On a mangé la dune. Montreal: Beauchemin, 1962.

Les Crasseux. Montreal: Holt, Rinehart and Winston, 1968.

Rabelais et les traditions populaires en Acadie. Quebec: Presses de l'Université Laval, 1971.

La Sagouine. Montreal: Leméac, 1971. *La Sagouine*. Trans. Luis de Céspedes. Toronto: Simon and Pierre, 1979.

Don l'Orignal. Montreal: Leméac, 1972. *The Tale of Don l'Orignal*. Trans. Barbara Godard. Toronto: Clarke, Irwin, 1978.

Par derrière chez mon père. Montreal: Leméac, 1972.

L'Acadie pour quasiment rien. With Rita Scalabrini. Montreal: Leméac, 1973.

Gapi et Sullivan. Montreal: Leméac, 1973. *Gapi and Sullivan*. Trans. Luis de Céspedes. Toronto: Simon and Pierre, 1987.

Mariaagélas. Montreal: Leméac, 1973. *Mariaagélas: Maria, Daughter of Gelas*. Trans. Ben-Z. Shek. Toronto: Simon and Pierre, 1986.

Emmanuel à Joseph à Dâvit. Montreal: Leméac, 1975.

Evangéline Deusse. Montreal: Leméac, 1975. *Evangeline the Second*. Trans. Luis de Céspedes. Toronto: Simon and Pierre, 1987.

Gapi. Montreal: Leméac, 1976.

Les Cordes-de-bois. Montreal: Leméac, 1977.

La Veuve enragée. Montreal: Leméac, 1977.

Le Bourgeois Gentleman. Montreal: Leméac, 1978.

Pélagie-la-Charrette. Montreal: Leméac, 1979. *Pélagie: The Return to a Homeland.* Trans. Philip Stratford. Garden City, NY: Doubleday, 1982.

Cents ans dans les bois. Montreal: Leméac, 1981. Republished as *La Gribouille.* Paris: Grasset, 1982.

Christophe Cartier de la Noisette dit Nounours. Paris: Hachette; Montreal: Leméac, 1981. *Christopher Cartier of Hazelnut, Also Known as Bear.* Trans. Wayne Grady. Toronto: Methuen, 1984.

La Contrebandière. Montreal: Leméac, 1981.

Les Drolatiques, Horrifiques et Epouvantables Aventures de Panurge, ami de Pantagruel, d'après Rabelais. Montreal: Leméac, 1983.

Les Acadiens, piétons de l'Atlantique. Et al. Paris: ACE, 1984.

Crache à pic. Montreal: Leméac, 1984. *The Devil is Loose!* Trans. Philip Stratford. Toronto: Lester and Orpen Dennys, 1986.

Garrochés en paradis. Montreal: Leméac, 1986.

Le Huitième Jour. Montreal: Leméac, 1986.

Margot la Folle. Montreal: Leméac, 1987.

WORKS ABOUT ANTONINE MAILLET

Aresu, Bernard. "Antonine Maillet and the Modern Epic." *Québec Studies* 4 (1986): 220-336.
Overview.

Aresu, Bernard. "*Pélagie-la-Charrette* and Antonine Maillet's Epic Voices." *Explorations: Essays in Comparative Literature.* Ed. Makoto Ueda. Lanham, MD: University Press of America, 1986. 211-26.
Overview.

Brown, Thomas H. "Maintaining Cultural Traditions Through Oral History: Antonine Maillet's *Pélagie-la-charrette.*" *Selected Proceedings of the Thirty-Fifth Annual Mountain Interstate Foreign Language Conference.* Ed. Raymon Fernandez-Rubio. Greenville, SC: Furman University, 1987. 71-77.
Discusses *Pélagie: The Return to a Homeland.*

Corbett, Lois. "The Very Best Tonine: Antonine Maillet's International Stature Hasn't Diverted the Author From Her Goal of Telling the Real Story of the Acadians." *Atlantic Insight* Sept. 1988: 14-16.
Interview.

Cowan, Doris. Interview. *Books in Canada* 11 May 1982: 24-26.

Czarnecki, Mark. "Prophet in Her Own Country Acadia." *Maclean's* 5 May 1980: 58-60+.
General.

Dinwoodie, Catriona. "Tentative Orality: The Role of *Pointe-aux-coques* and *On a mangé la dune* in Antonine Maillet's Search for a Narrative Strategy." *British Journal of Canadian Studies* 3.2 (1988): 234-43.

Downton, Dawn Rae. Rev. of *La Sagouine* by Antonine Maillet. *ArtsAtlantic* 7.4 (1987): 64-66.

Fitzpatrick, Marjorie A. "Antonine Maillet: The Search for a Narrative Voice." *Journal of Popular Culture* 15.3 (1981): 4-13.
Discusses *La Sagouine*, *Les Cordes-de-bois* and *Pélagie: The Return to a Homeland.*

Fitzpatrick, Marjorie A. "Antonine Maillet and the Epic Heroine." *Traditionalism, Nationalism, and Feminism: Women Writers of Quebec.* Ed. Paula Gilbert Lewis. Westport, CT: Greenwood, 1985. 141-55.
Discusses *Mariaagélas: Maria, Daughter of Gelas*, *Pélagie: The Return to a Homeland* and *Les Cordes-de-bois.*

Forsyth, Louise. "First Person Feminine Singular: Monologues by Women in Several Modern Quebec Plays." *Canadian Drama/L'art dramatique canadien* 5.2 (1979): 189-203.
Discusses *La Sagouine.*

Gleason, Marie. "*La Sagouine.*" *Atlantic Advocate* Apr. 1972: 55+.

Gobin, Pierre. "Space and Time in the Plays of Antonine Maillet." *Modern Drama* 25.1 (1982): 46-59.
Overview.

Godard, Barbara Thompson. "The Tale of a Narrative: Antonine Maillet's *Don l'Orignal.*" *Atlantis* 5.1 (1979): 51-69.
Discusses *The Tale of Don l'Orignal.*

Herz, Micheline. "A Québécois and an Acadian Novel Compared: The Use of Myth in Jovette Marchessault's *Comme une enfant de la terre* and Antonine Maillet's *Pélagie-la-Charrette.*" *Traditionalism, Nationalism, and Feminism: Women Writers of Quebec.* Ed. Paula Gilbert Lewis. Westport, CT: Greenwood, 1985. 173-83.
Discusses *Pélagie: The Return to a Homeland.*

Homel, David. "Profile: Antonine Maillet's Eternal Return of the Acadian Character." *Quill and Quire* June 1986: 37.
Discusses *The Devil is Loose!*

Howells, Robin. "*Pélagie-la-Charrette* and the Carnivalesque." *British Journal of Canadian Studies* 2.1 (1987): 48-60.
Discusses *Pélagie: The Return to a Homeland.*

Jacquot, Martine. "Last Story-teller: An Interview with Antonine Maillet." *Waves* 14.4 (1986): 93-95.

Keefer, Janice Kulyk. "Recent Maritime Fiction: Women and Words." *Studies in Canadian Literature* 11.2 (1986): 168-81.
Discusses *Mariaagélas: Maria, Daughter of Gelas.*

Keefer, Janice Kulyk. *Under Eastern Eyes: A Critical Reading of Maritime Fiction.* Toronto: University of Toronto Press, 1987. 116-22, 177-81.
Discusses *Pélagie: The Return to a Homeland, Mariaagélas: Maria, Daughter of Gelas* and *La Sagouine.*

Lacombe, Michèle. "Breaking the Silence of Centuries." *Canadian Theatre Review* 46 (1986): 58-64.
Overview.

Lacombe, Michèle. "Narrative, Carnival and Parody: Intertextuality in Antonine Maillet's *Pélagie-la-Charrette.*" *Canadian Literature* 116 (1988): 43-56.
Discusses *Pélagie: The Return to a Homeland.*

Lanken, Dane. "L'Acadienne." *Quest* Dec. 1982: 34-42.
Overview.

"Maillet Wins Prix Goncourt." *Quill and Quire* Jan. 1980: 1+.
Discusses *Pélagie: The Return to a Homeland.*

Mance, Douglas. "Acadjen, Eh? On Translating Acadian Literature." *Canadian Drama/L'art dramatique canadien* 2.2 (1976): 188-95.
Discusses *La Sagouine.*

May, Cedric. "Acadie Adieu." *Bulletin of Canadian Studies* 4.1 (1980): 75-83.
Discusses *Pélagie: The Return to a Homeland.*

May, Cedric. *Breaking the Silence: The Literature of Québec.* Birmingham, Eng.: University of Birmingham, Regional Studies Centre, 1981. 148-55.
Overview.

Moss, Jane. "Giants and Fat Ladies: Carnival Themes in Contemporary Quebec Theatre." *Québec Studies* 3 (1985): 160-68.
Discusses *Les Drolatiques, Horrifiques et Epouvantables Aventures de Panurge, ami de Pantagruel, d'après Rabelais.*

Pallister, Janis L. "Antonine Maillet: Spiritual Granddaughter of François Rabelais." *Québec Studies* 4 (1986): 261-85.
Overview.

Pallister, Janis L. "Antonine Maillet's *Evangéline Deusse*: Historical, Popular and Literary Elements." *American Review of Canadian Studies* 18.2 (1988): 239-48.
Discusses *Evangeline the Second.*

Paratte, Henri-Dominique. "Lonesome Travellers." *Books in Canada* Jan.-Feb. 1986: 6-8+.
Discusses *La Sagouine* and *Pélagie: The Return to a Homeland.*

Quinlan, James. "The Radical Dream of *Pélagie-la-Charrette.*" *Revue de l'Université Sainte-Anne* (1986): 24-31.
Discusses *Pélagie: The Return to a Homeland.*

Quinlan, James H. "*Pélagie-la-Charrette*: Spoken History in the Lyrical Novel." *Revue de l'Université Sainte-Anne* (1984-85): 32.
Discusses *Pélagie: The Return to a Homeland.*

Reid, Malcolm. "Carting Home the History of Acadia: The Unique Cultural Triumph of Antonine Maillet." *Saturday Night* May 1980: 23+.
General.

Shek, Ben-Z. "Antonine Maillet and the Prix Goncourt." *Canadian Modern Language Review* 36.3 (1980): 392-96.
Discusses *Pélagie: The Return to a Homeland.*

Shek, Ben-Zion. "Antonine Maillet: A Writer's Itinerary." *Acadiensis* 12.2 (1983): 171-80.
Overview.

Shouldice, Larry. "Antonine Maillet." *Canadian Writers Since 1960: Second Series*. Ed. W. H. New. Dictionary of Literary Biography 60. Detroit: Gale, 1987. 192-98.
Overview.

Slopen, Beverly. "The Literary Oscar...is the Affair of Fawcett Major?" *Quill and Quire* Apr. 1982: 21.
General.

Smith, Donald. "Antonine Maillet: Acadia, Land of Tales and Cunning." *Voices of Deliverance: Interviews with Quebec and Acadian Writers*. Trans. Larry Shouldice. Toronto: Anansi, 1986. 243-68.
Interview.

Smith, Donald. "Maillet and the Prix Goncourt." *Canadian Literature* 88 (1981): 157-61.
Overview.

Socken, Paul G. "The Bible and Myth in Antonine Maillet's *Pélagie-la-charrette*." *Studies in Canadian Literature* 12.2 (1987): 187-98.
Discusses *Pélagie: The Return to a Homeland.*

Stratford, Philip. "The Anatomy of a Translation: *Pélagie-la-Charrette*." *Translation in Canadian Literature*. Ed. Camille R. La Bossière. Ottawa: University of Ottawa Press, 1983. 121-30.
Discusses *Pélagie: The Return to a Homeland.*

Usmiani, Renate. "Recycling an Archetype: The Anti-Evangelines." *Canadian Theatre Review* 46 (1986): 65-71. Rpt. as "*Evangeline the Second*: Antonine Maillet's Archetype of Acadian Womanhood." *Evangeline the Second.* By Antonine Maillet. Trans. Luis de Céspedes. Toronto: Simon and Pierre, 1987. 11-17.
Overview.

Waterson, Karolyn. "The Mythical Dimension of *Pélagie-la-charrette*." *Francophone Literatures of the New World.* Ed. James P. Gilroy. Denver: University of Denver, Dept. of Foreign Languages and Literatures, 1982. 43-69.
Discusses *Pélagie: The Return to a Homeland.*

Webster, Jackie. "Antonine Maillet: First Lady of Acadian Literature." *Le Nouveau/New Brunswick* 5.2 (1980): 1-5.
Interview.

Webster, Jackie. "Antonine Maillet; Prizewinning Writer." *Chatelaine* Mar. 1981: 32.
General.

Weiss, Jonathan. "Toward a New Mythology: Antonine Maillet." *French-Canadian Theater.* Boston: Twayne, 1986. 94-106.
Overview.

Weiss, Jonathan M. "Acadia Transplanted: The Importance of Evangéline Deusse in the Work of Antonine Maillet." *Colby Library Quarterly* 13.3 (1977): 173-85.
Overview.

Wrenn, Phyllis. "Ortho- and Morpho-Graphic Transcoding of Acadian 'Franglais.'" *Visible Language* 21.1 (1987): 106-29.
Discusses *La Sagouine.*

BOOK REVIEWS

CENT ANS DANS LES BOIS

Canadian Literature 95 (1982): 172-75.
Dalhousie Review 61.3 (1981): 583-84.
French Review 56.3 (1983): 513-14.
World Literature Today 56.4 (1982): 646.

CHRISTOPHER CARTIER OF HAZELNUT, ALSO KNOWN AS BEAR/CHRISTOPHE CARTIER DE LA NOISETTE DIT NOUNOURS

Books in Canada Mar. 1985: 23.
Canadian Book Review Annual (1984): 337.
Canadian Children's Literature 41 (1986): 63.
Canadian Literature 96 (1983): 118-20.
Quarry 34.1 (1985): 84-85.
Quill and Quire Feb. 1985: 14.

LA CONTREBANDIERE

Canadian Literature 95 (1982): 137-40.

LES CORDES-DE-BOIS

Canadian Fiction Magazine 30-31 (1979): 217-20.
Canadian Literature 80 (1979): 76-78.
Quill and Quire Feb. 1978: 45.
World Literature Today 52.3 (1978): 429-30.

LES CRASSEUX

Journal of Canadian Fiction 3.3 (1974): 108-11.

THE DEVIL IS LOOSE!/CRACHE A PIC

Books in Canada Aug.-Sept. 1986: 16-17.
Canadian Forum Oct. 1986: 36-38.
Canadian Literature 105 (1985): 169-71.
Canadian Literature 115 (1987): 213-14.
Maclean's 26 May 1986: 52.
Quill and Quire Aug. 1986: 43.
University of Toronto Quarterly 57.1 (1987): 95-96.

LES DROLATIQUES, HORRIFIQUES ET EPOUVANTABLES AVENTURES DE PANURGE, AMI DE PANTAGRUEL, D'APRES RABELAIS

Canadian Literature 102 (1984): 98-101.
French Review 58.6 (1985): 919.

EVANGELINE THE SECOND/EVANGELINE DEUSSE

University of Toronto Quarterly 58.1 (1988): 86-87.

GAPI

Canadian Theatre Review 21 (1979): 142-43.

GAPI AND SULLIVAN/GAPI ET SULLIVAN

Journal of Canadian Fiction 3.3 (1974): 108-11.
University of Toronto Quarterly 58.1 (1988): 86-87.

GARROCHES EN PARADIS

Canadian Literature 119 (1988): 147-49.

LE HUITIEME JOUR

Canadian Literature 119 (1988): 147-49.

MARIAAGELAS: MARIA, DAUGHTER OF GELAS/MARIAAGELAS

Canadian Book Review Annual (1986): 81.
Canadian Forum Oct. 1986: 36-38.
Canadian Literature 119 (1988): 143-46.
Fiddlehead 151 (1987): 120-22.
Journal of Canadian Fiction 3.3 (1974): 108-11.
University of Toronto Quarterly 57.1 (1987): 95-96.

PELAGIE: THE RETURN TO A HOMELAND/PELAGIE-LA-CHARRETTE

Atlantic Advocate June 1982: 58.
Atlantic Monthly Apr. 1982: 108.
Books in Canada May 1982: 17+.
Canadian Fiction Magazine 34-35 (1980): 175-78.
Dalhousie Review 59.4 (1979-80): 764-65.
Essays on Canadian Writing 28 (1984): 156-59.
French Review 53.6 (1980): 978-79.
Maclean's 1 Mar. 1982: 57.
New York Times Book Review 7 Mar. 1982: 8+.
Quill and Quire Dec. 1979: 29-30.
Quill and Quire Apr. 1982: 28.
Saturday Night Mar. 1982: 54+.
Times Literary Supplement 3 Dec. 1982: 1344.
University of Toronto Quarterly 52.4 (1983): 386-88.

LA SAGOUINE

Books in Canada Apr. 1980: 13-14.
Branching Out 4.4 (1977): 43-44.
Brick 10 (1980): 23-24.
Canadian Book Review Annual (1982): 218.
Canadian Literature 91 (1981): 167-69.
Quill and Quire July 1979: 47-48.
University of Toronto Quarterly 49.4 (1980): 391-92.

THE TALE OF DON L'ORIGNAL/DON L'ORIGNAL

Canadian Book Review Annual (1978): 147.
Fiddlehead 124 (1980): 135-38.
University of Toronto Quarterly 49.4 (1980): 392-93.

LA VEUVE ENRAGEE

Canadian Literature 85 (1980): 129-30.

MARCHESSAULT, JOVETTE (1938-)

WORKS BY JOVETTE MARCHESSAULT

Comme une enfant de la terre/I: Le Crachat solaire. Montreal: Leméac, 1975. *Like a Child of the Earth*. Trans. Yvonne M. Klein. Vancouver: Talonbooks, 1988.

La Mère des herbes. Montreal: Quinze, 1980.

Triptyque lesbien. Montreal: Editions de la Pleine Lune, 1980. *Lesbian Triptych*. Trans. Yvonne M. Klein. Toronto: Women's Press, 1985.

La Saga des poules mouillées. Montreal: Editions de la Pleine Lune, 1981. *Saga of the Wet Hens*. Trans. Linda Gaboriau. Vancouver: Talonbooks, 1983.

Lettre de Californie. Montreal: Nouvelle Optique, 1982.

La Terre est trop courte, Violette Leduc. Montreal: Editions de la Pleine Lune, 1982.

Alice & Gertrude, Natalie & Renée et ce cher Ernest. Montreal: Editions de la Pleine Lune, 1984. "Alice and Gertrude and Natalie and Renée [sic] and dear Ernest." Trans. Basil Kingstone. *Canadian Fiction Magazine* 47 (1983): 58-64.

Anaïs, dans la queue de la comète. Montreal: Editions de la Pleine Lune, 1984.

Des cailloux blancs pour les forêts obscures. Montreal: Leméac, 1987.

WORKS ABOUT JOVETTE MARCHESSAULT

Forsyth, Louise H. "Women Reclaim Their Culture in Quebec: A Saga of Night Cows and Wet Hens." *Spirale* ns 1.2 (1981): 12-13+.
Discusses *Saga of the Wet Hens* and *Lesbian Triptych.*

Gaboriau, Linda. "Jovette Marchessault: A Luminous Wake in Space." *Canadian Theatre Review* 43 (1985): 91-99.
Overview.

Godard, Barbara. "Flying Away with Language." *Lesbian Triptych*. By Jovette Marchessault. Trans. Yvonne M. Klein. Toronto: Women's Press, 1985. 9-28.
Overview.

Green, Mary Jean, Paula Gilbert Lewis, and Karen Gould. "Inscriptions of the Feminine: A Century of Women Writing in Quebec." *American Review of Canadian Studies* 15.4 (1985): 363-88.
Discusses *La Mère des herbes*.

Hale, Amanda. "Voices, Vices and Voyeurs." Rev. of *The Edge of the Earth is Too Near*, *Violette Leduc* by Jovette Marchessault. *Broadside* June 1986: 11.

Herz, Micheline. "A Québécois and an Acadian Novel Compared: The Use of Myth in Jovette Marchessault's *Comme une enfant de la terre* and Antonine Maillet's *Pélagie-la-Charrette*." *Traditionalism, Nationalism, and Feminism: Women Writers of Quebec*. Ed. Paula Gilbert Lewis. Westport, CT: Greenwood, 1985. 173-83.
Discusses *Like a Child of the Earth*.

Kellett, Kathleen M. "Jovette Marchessault." *Canadian Writers Since 1960: Second Series*. Ed. W. H. New. Dictionary of Literary Biography 60. Detroit: Gale, 1987. 209-12.
Overview.

Marchessault, Jovette. Foreword. *Saga of the Wet Hens*. Trans. Linda Gaboriau. Vancouver: Talonbooks, 1983. 5-10.

Moss, Jane. "Creation Reenacted: The Woman Artist as Dramatic Figure." *American Review of Canadian Studies* 15.3 (1985): 263-72.
Discusses *Saga of the Wet Hens*, *Like a Child of the Earth* and *Alice and Gertrude and Natalie and Renée and dear Ernest*.

Moss, Jane. "Les Folles du Quebec: The Theme of Madness in Quebec Women's Theater." *French Review* 57.5 (1984): 617-24.
Discusses *Saga of the Wet Hens*.

Orenstein, Gloria. "The Telluric Women of Jovette Marchessault." Rev. of The Telluric Sculptures by Jovette Marchessault. *Fireweed* 5-6 (1979-80): 164-67.

Orenstein, Gloria Feman. "Jovette Marchessault: The Ecstatic Vision-Quest of the New Feminist Shaman." *Gynocritics: Feminist Approaches to Canadian and Quebec Women's Writing*. Ed. Barbara Godard. Toronto: ECW Press, 1987. 179-97.
Overview.

Orenstein, Gloria Feman. Postface. *Lesbian Triptych*. By Jovette Marchessault. Trans. Yvonne M. Klein. Toronto: Women's Press, 1985. 89-95.

Rosenfeld, Marthe. "The Development of a Lesbian Sensibility in the Work of Jovette Marchessault and Nicole Brossard." *Traditionalism, Nationalism and Feminism: Women Writers of Quebec*. Ed. Paula Gilbert Lewis. Westport, CT: Greenwood Press, 1985. 227-39.
Discusses *La Mère des herbes* and *Lesbian Triptych.*

Weiss, Jonathan M. "Quebec Theatre in the 80's: The End of an Era." *American Review of Canadian Studies* 13.2 (1983): 64-73.
Discusses *Saga of the Wet Hens.*

BOOK REVIEWS

ANAIS DANS LA QUEUE DE LA COMETE

French Review 60.5 (1987): 728-29.

LESBIAN TRIPTYCH/TRIPTYQUE LESBIEN

Books in Canada Aug.-Sept. 1985: 25.
Broadside May 1985: 13.
Canadian Book Review Annual (1985): 213-14.
Canadian Literature 112 (1987): 128-29.
New Statesman 12 July 1985: 28.
Resources for Feminist Research/Documentation sur la recherche feministe 15.4 (1986-1987): 61.
University of Toronto Quarterly 56.1 (1986): 81-82.

LA MERE DES HERBES

World Literature Today 55.4 (1981): 639-40.

SAGA OF THE WET HENS/LA SAGA DES POULES MOUILLEES

Books in Canada Apr. 1984: 14.
Canadian Book Review Annual (1983): 257-58.
French Review 56.5 (1983): 788-89.
Quill and Quire Apr. 1984: 33.
University of Toronto Quarterly 53.4 (1984): 409-10.

MARTIN, CLAIRE (1914-)

WORKS BY CLAIRE MARTIN

Avec ou sans amour. Montreal: Cercle du Livre de France, 1958. *Love Me, Love Me Not*. Trans. David Lobdell. Ottawa: Oberon, 1987.

Doux-amer. Montreal: Cercle du Livre de France, 1960. *Best Man*. Trans. David Lobdell. Ottawa: Oberon, 1983.

Quand j'aurai payé ton visage. Montreal: Cercle du Livre de France, 1962. *The Legacy*. Trans. David Lobdell. Ottawa: Oberon, 1986.

Dans un gant de fer. Montreal: Cercle du Livre de France, 1965. *In an Iron Glove*. Trans. Philip Stratford. Toronto: Ryerson Press, 1968. *In an Iron Glove*: *An Autobiography*. Trans. Philip Stratford. Montreal: Harvest House, 1975.

La Joue droite. Montreal: Cercle du Livre de France, 1966. *In an Iron Glove*. Trans. Philip Stratford. Toronto: Ryerson Press, 1968. *The Right Cheek*: *An Autobiography*. Trans. Philip Stratford. Montreal: Harvest House, 1975.

Les Morts. Montreal: Cercle du Livre de France, 1970.

"Moi, je n'étais qu'espoir." Montreal: Cercle du Livre de France, 1972.

La Petite Fille lit. Ottawa: Presses de l'Université d'Ottawa, 1973.

La Belle histoire. Hull, Que.: Editions E.L.V.O., 1985.

Faux départ. Hull, Que.: Editions E.L.V.O., 1985.

WORKS ABOUT CLAIRE MARTIN

Bassett, Isabel. "Women in Quebec." *The Parlour Rebellion: Profiles in the Struggle for Women's Rights*. Toronto: McClelland and Stewart, 1975. 186-92.
Biographical.

Brazeau, J. Raymond. "Claire Martin." *An Outline of Contemporary French Canadian Literature*. Toronto: Forum House, 1972. 49-58.
Discusses *Love Me, Love Me Not*, *The Legacy* and *Best Man*.

Green, Mary Jean. "Structures of Liberation: Female Experience and Autobiographical Form in Quebec." *Yale French Studies* 65 (1983): 124-36.
Discusses *In an Iron Glove*.

Hesse, M. G. "A Comparative Study of Claire Martin's *Dans un gant de fer* and *La joue droite* and Percy Jane's *House of Hate*." *Journal of Canadian Fiction* 3.2 (1974): 77-81.
Discusses *In an Iron Glove* and *The Right Cheek*.

Mitcham, Allison. "Women in Revolt: Anne Hébert's, Marie-Claire Blais' and Claire Martin's Nightmare Vision of an Unjust Society." *Alive Magazine* 3.29 (1973): 13-14.
Discusses *In an Iron Glove*.

Rackowski, Cheryl Stokes. *Women by Women: Five Contemporary English and French Canadian Novelists*. Diss. University of Connecticut, 1978.
Discusses *Best Man*.

Stratford, Philip, trans. Translator's Preface. *In an Iron Glove*. By Claire Martin. Toronto: Ryerson Press, 1968. v-vi.

Tougas, Gérard. *History of French-Canadian Literature*. Trans. Alta Lind Cook. 2nd ed. Toronto: Ryerson Press, 1966. 193.
Discusses *The Legacy*, *Love Me, Love Me Not* and *Best Man*.

Urbas, Jeanette. "Oppression of Children." *From* Thirty Acres *to Modern Times: The Story of French-Canadian Literature*. Toronto: McGraw-Hill Ryerson, 1976. 93-99.
Discusses *In an Iron Glove*.

Weir, Lorraine. "Claire Martin." *Canadian Writers Since 1960: Second Series*. Ed. W. H. New. Dictionary of Literary Biography 60. Detroit: Gale, 1987. 222-25.
Overview.

BOOK REVIEWS

BEST MAN/DOUX-AMER

Books in Canada Aug.-Sept. 1983: 29.
Brick 20 (1984): 15-16.
Canadian Book Review Annual (1983): 176-77.
Quill and Quire July 1983: 56.
University of Toronto Quarterly 53.4 (1984): 403.

IN AN IRON GLOVE/DANS UN GANT DE FER; LA JOUE DROITE

Brick 2 (1978): 11-12.
Canadian Literature 42 (1969): 82-84.
Commentator July-Aug. 1969: 30.
Tamarack Review 52 (1969): 80-82.

THE LEGACY/QUAND J'AURAI PAYE TON VISAGE

Canadian Literature 119 (1988): 143-46.
Cross-Canada Writers' Quarterly 9.2 (1987): 24-25.
Fiddlehead 152 (1987): 95-98.
Queen's Quarterly 94.2 (1987): 366-75.
Quill and Quire Sept. 1986: 82.

LOVE ME, LOVE ME NOT/AVEC OU SANS AMOUR

Dalhousie Review 67.2-3 (1987): 377-79.
University of Toronto Quarterly 58.1 (1988): 92-93.

MIRON, GASTON (1928-)

WORKS BY GASTON MIRON

Deux Sangs. With Olivier Marchand. Montreal: L'Hexagone, 1953.

L'Homme rapaillé. Montreal: Presses de l'Université de Montréal, 1970. *The Agonized Life*. Ed. and trans. Marc Plourde. Montreal: Torchy Wharf Press, 1980. *Embers and Earth*: *Selected Poems*. Trans. D. G. Jones and Marc Plourde. Bilingual ed. Montreal: Guernica, 1984.

Courtepointes. Ottawa: Editions de l'Université d'Ottawa, 1975.

La Marche à l'amour. Montreal: Erta, 1977. *The March to Love*: *Selected Poems*. Ed. Douglas G. Jones. Trans. Douglas G. Jones et al. Pittsburgh, PA: International Poetry Forum, 1986.

WORKS ABOUT GASTON MIRON

Beaulieu, Michel. "Miron, the Publisher-Poet." *Quill and Quire* Nov. 1979: 8.
General.

Beaver, John. "Gaston Miron." *The Language of Poetry*: *Crisis and Solution*: *Studies in Modern Poetry of French Expression*, *1945 to the Present*. Ed. Michael Bishop. Amsterdam: Rodopi, 1980. 229-54.
Overview.

Bednarski, Betty. "The Humiliations of Canadian French." *Times Literary Supplement* 26 Oct. 1973: 1317.
General.

Brault, Jacques. "Gaston Miron, Politics or Poetry." Trans. Barbara Belyea. *Ellipse* 6 (1971): 54-58.
Discusses poetry.

Chamberland, Paul. "Founding the Territory." *Contemporary Quebec Criticism*. Ed. and trans. Larry Shouldice. Toronto: University of Toronto Press, 1979. 148-50.
General.

Cloutier-Wojciechowska, Cécile. "Gaston Miron." *Canadian Writers Since 1960: Second Series*. Ed. W. H. New. Dictionary of Literary Biography 60. Detroit: Gale, 1987. 250-54.
Overview.

"Editorial." *Ellipse* 5 (1970): 6-7.
General.

D'Alfonso, Antonio. "Gaston Miron in Rome: Quebec." *Poetry Canada Review* 6.4 (1985): 18.
General.

Gervais, Guy. Introduction. *The March to Love: Selected Poems*. By Gaston Miron. Ed. Douglas G. Jones. Trans. Douglas G. Jones et al. Pittsburgh, PA: International Poetry Forum, 1986. i-iii.

Jones, D. G. "Gaston Miron: A Testimony." *Ellipse* 5 (1970): 55-57. Rpt. in *Embers and Earth: Selected Poems*. By Gaston Miron. Trans. D. G. Jones and Marc Plourde. Montreal: Guernica, 1984. 7-9.

Lee, Veronica. "Gaston Miron and a Strategy for Writing." *British Journal of Canadian Studies* 3.2 (1988): 244-58.
Discusses *L'Homme rapaillé*.

May, Cedric. "Self and Non-Self: The Sense of Otherness in Quebec Poetry." *Bulletin of Canadian Studies* 2.2 (1978): 52-63.
Discusses poetry.

Picotte, Jacques. "Miron, the Anthropoet." *The Agonized Life*. By Gaston Miron. Ed. and trans. Marc Plourde. Montreal: Torchy Wharf Press, 1980. 73-78.
Interview.

Plourde, Marc. "On Translating Miron." *Embers and Earth: Selected Poems*. By Gaston Miron. Montreal: Guernica, 1984. 113-22. Rpt. in *The Insecurity of Art: Essays on Poetics*. Ed. Ken Norris and Peter Van Toorn. Montreal: Vehicule, 1982. 108-14.

Vachon, G.-André. "Gaston Miron, or the Invention of Substance." Trans. Cormac Gerard Cappon. *Ellipse* 5 (1970): 38-54.
Discusses *Deux Sangs.*

BOOK REVIEWS

THE AGONIZED LIFE/L'HOMME RAPAILLE

Books in Canada Feb. 1981: 16-17.
Canadian Book Review Annual (1981): 168.
Canadian Forum Nov. 1980: 35.
Quarry 30.1 (1981): 79-82.
Queen's Quarterly 89.1 (1982): 217-20.
University of Toronto Quarterly 50.4 (1981): 90-91.

EMBERS AND EARTH/L'HOMME RAPAILLE

Antigonish Review 1.3 (1970): 126-29.
Poetry Canada Review 6.4 (1985): 29.
Quarry 35.3 (1986): 103-07.
Rubicon 5 (1985): 138-42.
University of Toronto Quarterly 54.4 (1985): 395-96.

NELLIGAN, EMILE (1879-1941)

WORKS BY EMILE NELLIGAN

Emile Nelligan et son oeuvre. Montreal: Beachemin, 1903; 2nd ed. Garand, 1925; 3rd ed. Imprimerie Excelsior, 1932; 4th ed. Fides, 1945.

Poésies complètes, 1896-1899. Montreal: Fides, 1952; 2nd ed. 1958; 3rd ed. 1966. *The Complete Poems of Emile Nelligan*. Trans. Fred Cogswell. Montreal: Harvest House, 1983.

Selected Poems. Trans. P. F. Widdows. Toronto: Ryerson Press, 1960.

Poésies. Montreal: Fides, 1967.

Pour un plaisir de verbe: carnets et cahiers d'Emile Nelligan. Ed. Bernard Courteau. Montreal: Editions Emile-Nelligan, 1982.

31 poèmes autographes: 2 carnets d'hôpital, 1938. Trois-Rivières, Que.: Ecrits des Forges, 1982.

WORKS ABOUT EMILE NELLIGAN

Abley, Mark, trans. Translator's Note. "A Lighted Match: Seven Poems Translated from the French of Emile Nelligan by Mark Abley." *Northern Light* 9 (1983): 38-39.

Bourassa, André G. *Surrealism and Quebec Literature*. Trans. Mark Czarnecki. Toronto: University of Toronto Press, 1984. 9-11.
Discusses *The Complete Poems*.

Cogswell, Fred, trans. "Emile Nelligan." *The Complete Poems of Emile Nelligan*. By Emile Nelligan. Montreal: Harvest House, 1983. xvii-xxiv.

"Emile Nelligan." *Saturday Night* 13 Dec. 1941: 3.
Obituary.

Jones, D. G. "Grounds for Translation." *Ellipse* 21 (1977): 58-90. Rpt. in *The Insecurity of Art: Essays on Poetics*. Ed. Ken Norris and Peter van Toorn. Montreal: Vehicule Press, 1982. 67-80.
Discusses *The Complete Poems*.

Lewis, Paula Gilbert. "Emile Nelligan: 'Poète maudite' of Quebec: The Pervasion of Black and White and Coldness." *Pre/Text/Text/Context: Essays on Nineteenth-Century French Literature*. Ed. Robert L. Mitchell. Columbus, OH: Ohio State University Press, 1980. 229-36.
Discusses *The Complete Poems*.

May, Cedric. *Breaking the Silence: The Literature of Québec*. Birmingham, Eng.: University of Birmingham, Regional Canadian Studies Centre, 1981. 41-50.
Discusses *The Complete Poems*.

Mezei, Kathy. "Emile Nelligan: A Dreamer Passing By." *Canadian Literature* 87 (1980): 81-99.
Discusses *The Complete Poems*.

Mezei, Kathy. "Lampman and Nelligan: Dream Landscapes." *Canadian Review of Comparative Literature* 6.2 (1979): 151-65.
Discusses *The Complete Poems*.

Mezei, Kathy. *A Magic Space Wherein the Mind Can Dwell: Place and Space in the Poetry of Archibald Lampman, Emile Nelligan, and Duncan Campbell Scott*. Diss. Queen's University, 1977.
Discusses *The Complete Poems*.

Montigny, Louvigny de. "Emile Nelligan and the Ecole Littéraire de Montréal." *Saturday Night* 1 Nov. 1947: 32.
Discusses *The Complete Poems*.

Tougas, Gérard. *History of French-Canadian Literature*. Trans. Alta Lind Cook. 2nd ed. Toronto: Ryerson Press, 1966. 73-76.
Discusses *The Complete Poems*.

Widdows, P. F., trans. Introduction. *Selected Poems*. By Emile Nelligan. Toronto: Ryerson Press, 1960. v-xi.

Wilson, Edmund. *O Canada: An American's Notes on Canadian Culture*. New York: Farrar, Straus and Giroux, 1964. 97-101.
Discusses *The Complete Poems.*

Wright, Percy H. "Canada's Boy Poet." *Saturday Night* 17 Dec. 1938: 26.
Discusses *The Complete Poems.*

BOOK REVIEWS

THE COMPLETE POEMS OF EMILE NELLIGAN/POESIES COMPLETES, 1896-1899

Canadian Book Review Annual (1983): 225.
Canadian Literature 102 (1984): 153-54.
Fiddlehead 143 (1985): 93-98.
University of Toronto Quarterly 53.4 (1984): 396-98.

SELECTED POEMS

Canadian Forum July 1961: 92.
Fiddlehead 48 (1961): 53.
Tamarack Review 23 (1962): 100-01.
University of Toronto Quarterly 30.4 (1961): 400-01.

RINGUET (1895-1960)
(Pseud. of Philippe Panneton)

WORKS BY RINGUET

Littératures à la manière de... With Louis Francoeur. Montreal: Edouard Garand, 1924.

30 Arpents. Paris: Flammarion, 1928. *Thirty Acres*. Trans. Felix and Dorothea Walter. Toronto: Macmillan, 1940.

Un Monde était leur empire. Montreal: Editions Variétés, 1943.

L'Héritage et autres contes. Montreal: Editions Variétés, 1946.

Fausse Monnaie. Montreal: Editions Variétés, 1947.

Le Poids du jour. Montreal: Editions Variétés, 1949.

L'Amiral et le facteur: ou, comment l'Amérique ne fut pas découverte. Montreal: Dussault, 1954.

Confidences. Montreal: Fides, 1965.

WORKS ABOUT RINGUET

Atwood, Margaret. *Survival: A Thematic Guide to Canadian Literature*. Toronto: Anansi, 1972. 136, 218-19.
Discusses *Thirty Acres*.

Bladen, V. W. "Lorne Pierce Medal [Presented to] Philippe Panneton." *Royal Society of Canada. Transactions* 3rd ser. 53 (1959): 50.
General.

Cagnon, Maurice. *The French Novel of Quebec*. Boston: Twayne, 1986. 27-29.
Discusses *Thirty Acres*.

Cogswell, Fred. "The French Canadian Novel and the Problem of Social Change." *Journal of Canadian Fiction* 1.2 (1972): 65-68.
Discusses *Thirty Acres.*

Dorsinville, Max. *Caliban Without Prospero: Essay on Quebec and Black Literature.* Erin, Ont.: Porcépic, 1974. 59-75.
Discusses *Thirty Acres.*

"Fruitful Vice." *Time* (*Can. ed.*) 19 Dec. 1949: 16.
Discusses *Thirty Acres* and *Le Poids du jour.*

Hoekema, H. "The Illusion of Realism in *Thirty Acres.*" *Essays on Canadian Writing* 17 (1980): 102-12.

Laflèche, Guy. "Ringuet's *Trente arpents*: For Different Men But Always the Same Literature." Trans. Erec Koch. *Yale French Studies* 65 (1983): 155-71.
Discusses *Thirty Acres.*

Legrand, Albert. Introduction. *Thirty Acres.* By Philippe Panneton. Trans. Felix and Dorothea Walter. New Canadian Library 12. Toronto: McClelland and Stewart, 1960. ix-xiv.

Miller, Wm. Marion. "Ringuet, French Canadian Novelist." *Books Abroad* 26 (1952): 26-29.
Overview.

Shek, Ben-Zion. *Social Realism in the French-Canadian Novel.* Montreal: Harvest House, 1977. 56-59, 157-69.
Discusses *Thirty Acres* and *Le Poids du jour.*

Sirois, Antoine. "Ringuet." *Canadian Writers, 1920-1959: First Series.* Ed. W. H. New. Dictionary of Literary Biography 68. Detroit: Gale, 1988. 290-94.
Overview.

Sirois, Antoine. "Ringuet." Trans. E. A. Walker. *Profiles in Canadian Literature.* Ed. Jeffrey M. Heath. Toronto: Dundurn Press, 1982. 3: 81-88.
Overview.

Socken, Paul. "The Narrative Structure of *Trente Arpents.*" *Canadian Literature* 86 (1980): 152-56.
Discusses *Thirty Acres.*

Sutherland, Ronald. *Second Image: Comparative Studies in Quebec/Canadian Literature.* Toronto: New Press, 1971. 6-10.
Discusses *Thirty Acres.*

Sutherland, Ronald. "Twin Solitudes." *Canadian Literature* 31 (1967): 5-24.
Discusses *Thirty Acres.*

Talbot, Emile J. "Communication and Culture in *Trente arpents.*" *American Review of Canadian Studies* 14.3 (1984): 291-97.
Discusses *Thirty Acres.*

Tougas, Gérard. *History of French-Canadian Literature.* Trans. Alta Lind Cook. 2nd ed. Toronto: Ryerson Press, 1966. 131-32.
Discusses *Thirty Acres.*

Urbas, Jeanette. "Undermining the Myth." *From* Thirty Acres *to Modern Times: The Story of French-Canadian Literature.* Toronto: McGraw-Hill Ryerson, 1976. 19-31.
Discusses *Thirty Acres.*

Warwick, Jack. *The Long Journey: Literary Themes of French Canada.* Toronto: University of Toronto Press, 1968. 130-35.
Discusses *Un Monde était leur empire, Fausse Monnaie* and *Thirty Acres.*

BOOK REVIEWS

L'AMIRAL ET LE FACTEUR

University of Toronto Quarterly 24.3 (1955): 329.

FAUSSE MONNAIE

University of Toronto Quarterly 17.4 (1948): 404-05.

L'HERITAGE ET AUTRES CONTES

University of Toronto Quarterly 16.3 (1947): 277.

LE POIDS DU JOUR

University of Toronto Quarterly 19.4 (1950): 399-401.

THIRTY ACRES/TRENTE ARPENTS

Canadian Forum Jan. 1941: 323-24.
Dalhousie Review 20 (1941): 519-20.
New York Times Book Review 19 Mar. 1939: 8+.
New York Times Book Review 7 Jan. 1940: 8+.
New York Times Book Review 13 Oct. 1940: 6-7.
Queen's Quarterly 47.4 (1940): 489-90.
Saturday Night 23 Nov. 1940: 19.
Times Literary Supplement 14 Dec. 1940: 629.
University of Toronto Quarterly 8.4 (1939): 480-81.

ROY, GABRIELLE (1909-1983)

WORKS BY GABRIELLE ROY

Bonheur d'occasion. 2 vols. Montreal: Société des Editions Pascal, 1945; rev. Paris: Flammarion, 1947. *The Tin Flute*. Trans. Hannah Josephson. Toronto: McClelland and Stewart, 1947. *The Tin Flute*. Trans. Alan Brown. Toronto: McClelland and Stewart, 1980.

La Petite Poule d'eau. Montreal: Beauchemin, 1950. *Where Nests the Water Hen*. Trans. Harry Lorin Binsse. Toronto: McClelland and Stewart, 1951.

Alexandre Chenevert. Montreal: Beauchemin, 1954. *The Cashier*. Trans. Harry Lorin Binsse. Toronto: McClelland and Stewart, 1955.

Rue Deschambault. Montreal: Beauchemin, 1955. *Street of Riches*. Trans. Harry Lorin Binsse. Toronto: McClelland and Stewart, 1957.

La Montagne secrète. Montreal: Beauchemin, 1961. *The Hidden Mountain*. Trans. Harry Lorin Binsse. Toronto: McClelland and Stewart, 1962.

La Route d'Altamont. Montreal: HMH, 1966. *The Road Past Altamont*. Trans. Joyce Marshall. Toronto: McClelland and Stewart, 1966.

La Rivière sans repos. Montreal: Beauchemin, 1970. *Windflower*. Abr. ed. Trans. Joyce Marshall. Toronto: McClelland and Stewart, 1970.

Cet été qui chantait. Quebec: Editions Françaises, 1972. *Enchanted Summer*. Trans. Joyce Marshall. Toronto: McClelland and Stewart, 1976.

Un Jardin au bout du monde et autres nouvelles. Montreal: Beauchemin, 1975. *Garden in the Wind*. Trans. Alan Brown. Toronto: McClelland and Stewart, 1977.

Ma Vache Bossie. Montreal: Leméac, 1976.

Ces Enfants de ma vie. Montreal: Stanké, 1977. *Children of My Heart*. Trans. Alan Brown. Toronto: McClelland and Stewart, 1979.

Fragiles lumières de la terre: écrits divers, 1942-1970. Montreal: Quinze, 1978. *The Fragile Lights of Earth: Articles and Memories, 1942-1970*. Trans. Alan Brown. Toronto: McClelland and Stewart, 1982.

Courte-Queue. Montreal: Stanké, 1979. *Cliptail*. Trans. Alan Brown. Toronto: McClelland and Stewart, 1980.

De quoi t'ennuies-tu, Eveline? Montreal: Editions du Sentier, 1982.

De quoi t'ennuies-tu, Eveline? suivi de Ely! Ely! Ely! Montreal: Boréal, 1984.

La Détresse et l'enchantement. Montreal: Boréal, 1984. *Enchantment and Sorrow: The Autobiography of Gabrielle Roy*. Trans. Patricia Claxton. Toronto: Lester and Orpen Dennys, 1987.

La Pékinoise et l'Espagnole. Montreal: Stanké, 1987.

Ma Chère petite soeur: lettres à Bernadette, 1943-1970. Ed. François Ricard. Montreal: Boréal, 1988.

WORKS ABOUT GABRIELLE ROY

Abley, Mark. "A Messenger of Hope." *Maclean's* 25 July 1983: 55.
Obituary.

Atwood, Margaret. *Survival: A Thematic Guide to Canadian Literature*. Toronto: Anansi, 1972. 80, 191, 219-20, 223.
Discusses *The Hidden Mountain* and *The Tin Flute*.

Babby, Ellen R. "*Alexandre Chenevert*: Prisoner of Language." *Modern Language Studies* 12.2 (1982): 22-30.
Discusses *The Cashier*.

Babby, Ellen R. *The Language of Spectacle and the Spectacle of Language in Selected Texts of Gabrielle Roy*. Diss. Yale University, 1980.
Discusses *The Tin Flute*, *Windflower* and *The Cashier*.

Babby, Ellen R. *The Play of Language and Spectacle: A Structural Reading of Selected Texts by Gabrielle Roy*. Toronto: ECW Press, 1985.
Discusses *The Tin Flute*, *Windflower* and *The Cashier*.

Babby, Ellen R. "*La Rivière sans repos*: Gabrielle Roy's 'Spectacular' Text." *Québec Studies* 2 (1984): 105-17.
Discusses *Windflower*.

Blodgett, E. D. "Gardens at the World's End or Gone West in French." *Essays on Canadian Writing* 17 (1980): 113-26.
Discusses *The Road Past Altamont*.

Brazeau, J. Raymond. "Gabrielle Roy." *An Outline of Contemporary French Canadian Literature*. Toronto: Forum House, 1972. 11-20.
Discusses *The Road Past Altamont* and *Street of Riches*.

Brotherson, Lee. "*Alexandre Chenevert*: An Unhappy Sisyphus." *Essays in French Literature* 18 (1981): 86-99.
Discusses *The Cashier*.

Brown, Alan G. "Gabrielle Roy and the Temporary Provincial." *Tamarack Review* 1 (1976): 61-70.
Overview.

Cagnon, Maurice. *The French Novel of Quebec*. Boston: Twayne, 1986. 34-41.
Overview.

Cameron, Donald. "Gabrielle Roy: A Bird in the Prison Window." *Conversations With Canadian Novelists*. Toronto: Macmillan, 1973. Pt. 2: 128-45.
Interview.

Chadbourne, Richard. "The Journey in Gabrielle Roy's Novels." *Travel, Quest, and Pilgrimage as a Literary Theme: Studies in Honor of Reino Virtanen*. Ed. Frans C. Amelinckx and Joyce N. Megay. Manhatten, KS: Society of Spanish and Spanish-American Studies, 1978. 251-60.
Overview.

Chadbourne, Richard. "Two Visions of the Prairies: Willa Cather and Gabrielle Roy." *The New Land: Studies in a Literary Theme*. Ed. Richard Chadbourne and Hallvard Dahlie. Waterloo, Ont.: Wilfrid Laurier University Press, 1978. 93-120.
Overview.

Clark, J. Wilson. "Pro-Imperialist Ideas in Gabrielle Roy's *Tin Flute*." *Literature and Ideology* 13 (1972): 31-40.

Claxton, Patricia, trans. Translator's Note. *Enchantment and Sorrow: The Autobiography of Gabrielle Roy*. By Gabrielle Roy. Toronto: Lester and Orpen Dennys, 1987. vii-x.

Cobb, David. "I Have, I think, a Grateful Heart." *Canadian Magazine* 1 May 1976: 10-14.
Interview.

Cogswell, Fred. "The French Canadian Novel and the Problem of Social Change." *Journal of Canadian Fiction* 1.2 (1972): 65-68.
Discusses *The Cashier*.

Conron, Brandon. Introduction. *Street of Riches*. By Gabrielle Roy. Trans. Harry Lorin Binsse. New Canadian Library 56. Toronto: McClelland and Stewart, 1967. vii-xii.

Davidson, Arnold E. "Gabrielle Roy's *Where Nests the Water Hen*: An Island Beyond the Waste Land." *North Dakota Quarterly* 47.4 (1979): 4-10.

Delson-Karan, Myrna. *An Analysis of Selected Novels of the French-Canadian Writer, Gabrielle Roy* (*Volumes I and II*). Diss. New York University, 1985.
Overview.

Dorsinville, Max. *Caliban Without Prospero*: *Essay on Quebec and Black Literature*. Erin, Ont.: Porcépic, 1974. 105-33.
Discusses *The Tin Flute*.

Dufault, Roseanna. "Personal and Political Childhood in Quebec: Analogies for Identity." *Continental, Latin-American and Francophone Women Writers*. Ed. Eunice Myers and Ginette Adamson. Lanham, MD: UP of America, 1987. 63-69.
Discusses *Street of Riches*.

Duncan, Dorothy. "Le Triomphe de Gabrielle." *Maclean's* 15 Apr. 1947: 23+.
Interview.

Edwards, Mary Jane. Introduction. *The Hidden Mountain*. By Gabrielle Roy. Trans. Harry Lorin Binsse. New Canadian Library 109. Toronto: McClelland and Stewart, 1974. n. pag.

Ewing, Ronald. "Two Solitudes and *Bonheur d'occasion*: Mirror Images of Quebec." *Journal of Canadian Culture* 2.2 (1985): 85-98.
Discusses *The Tin Flute*.

Fairley, Margaret. "Gabrielle Roy's Novels." *New Frontiers* 5.1 (1956): 7-10.
Discusses *The Cashier*, *Where Nests the Water Hen* and *The Tin Flute*.

Fiand, Barbara. "Gabrielle Roy's *The Hidden Mountain*: A Poetic Expression of Existential Thought." *Malahat Review* 52 (1979): 77-85.

Fitzpatrick, Marjorie A. "Teaching French-Canadian Civilization Through the Literature: Hémon, Roy, and Blais." *Québec Studies* 2 (1984): 82-93.
Discusses *The Tin Flute*.

Grace, Sherrill E. "Quest for the Peaceable Kingdom: Urban/Rural Codes in Roy, Laurence, and Atwood." *Women Writers and the City: Essays in Feminist Literary Criticism*. Ed. Susan Merrill Squier. Knoxville: University of Tennessee, 1984. 193-209.
Discusses *The Tin Flute*.

Grady, Wayne. "Gabrielle Roy." *Today* 5 Dec. 1981: 11.
General.

Green, Mary Jean. "Gabrielle Roy and Germaine Guèvremont: Quebec's Daughters Face a Changing World." *Journal of Women's Studies in Literature* 1.3 (1979): 243-57.
Discusses *The Tin Flute*.

Green, Mary Jean, Paula Gilbert Lewis, and Karen Gould. "Inscriptions of the Feminine: A Century of Women Writing in Quebec." *American Review of Canadian Studies* 15.4 (1985): 363-88.
Overview.

Grosskurth, Phyllis. *Gabrielle Roy*. Toronto: Forum House, 1969.
Overview.

Grosskurth, Phyllis. "Gabrielle Roy and the Silken Noose." *Canadian Literature* 42 (1969): 6-13.
General.

Hayne, David M. "Gabrielle Roy." *Canadian Modern Language Review* 13.2 (1957): 5-11. Rpt. in *Canadian Modern Language Review* 21.1 (1964): 20-26.
Overview.

Hesse, M. G. *Gabrielle Roy*. Boston: Twayne, 1984.
Overview.

Hesse, M. G. "Mothers and Daughters in Gabrielle Roy's *The Tin Flute*, *Street of Riches* and *The Road Past Altamont*." *Journal of Canadian Culture* 2.1 (1985): 89-100.

Hesse, M. G. "There Are No More Strangers: Gabrielle Roy's Immigrants." *Canadian Children's Literature* 35-36 (1984): 27-37.
Overview.

Hind-Smith, Joan. "Gabrielle Roy." *Three Voices: The Lives of Margaret Laurence, Gabrielle Roy, Frederick Philip Grove*. Toronto: Clarke, Irwin, 1975. 62-126.
Biographical.

Homel, David. "Gabrielle Roy, 1909-1983." *Books in Canada* Aug.-Sept. 1983: 12.
Obituary.

Hoy, Helen. "Gabrielle Roy." *Canadian Writers, 1920-1959: First Series*. Ed. W. H. New. Dictionary of Literary Biography 68. Detroit: Gale, 1988. 299-317.
Overview.

Jain, Sashil Kumar. "Gabrielle Roy: A French-Canadian Novelist." *Culture* 31 (1970): 391-99.
Overview.

Lacombe, Michèle. "The Origins of *The Hidden Mountain*." *Canadian Literature* 88 (1981): 164-66.

Lafontaine, Cecile. "L'étrangère: Gabrielle Roy's Search for Home." *Canadian Forum* May 1986: 16-22.
Discusses *Enchantment and Sorrow*.

Lewis, Paula Gilbert. "Female Spirals and Male Cages: The Urban Sphere in the Novels of Gabrielle Roy." *Traditionalism, Nationalism, and Feminism: Women Writers of Quebec*. Ed. Paula Gilbert Lewis. Westport, CT: Greenwood, 1985. 71-81.
Overview.

Lewis, Paula Gilbert. "Feminism and Traditionalism in the Early Short Stories of Gabrielle Roy." *Traditionalism, Nationalism, and Feminism: Women Writers of Quebec*. Ed. Paula Gilbert Lewis. Westport, CT: Greenwood, 1985. 27-35.

Lewis, Paula Gilbert. "The Fragility of Childhood: Gabrielle Roy's *Ces enfants de ma vie*." *American Review of Canadian Studies* 9.2 (1979): 148-53.
Discusses *Children of My Heart*.

Lewis, Paula Gilbert. "Gabrielle Roy and Emile Zola: French Naturalism in Quebec." *Modern Language Studies* 11.3 (1981): 44-50.
Overview.

Lewis, Paula Gilbert. "Gabrielle Roy, 1909-1983." *American Review of Canadian Studies* 13.2 (1983): vi.
Obituary.

Lewis, Paula Gilbert. "The Incessant Call of the Open Road: Gabrielle Roy's Incorrigible Nomads." *French Review* 53.6 (1980): 816-25.
Overview.

Lewis, Paula Gilbert. "The Last of the Great Storytellers: A Visit With Gabrielle Roy." *French Review* 55.2 (1981): 207-15.
Interview.

Lewis, Paula Gilbert. *The Literary Vision of Gabrielle Roy: An Analysis of Her Works*. Birmingham, AL: Summa, 1984.
Overview.

Lewis, Paula Gilbert. "The Resignation of Old Age, Sickness and Death in the Fiction of Gabrielle Roy." *American Review of Canadian Studies* 11.2 (1981): 49-66.
Overview.

Lewis, Paula Gilbert. "*Street of Riches* and *The Road Past Altamont*: The Feminine World of Gabrielle Roy." *Journal of Women's Studies in Literature* 1.2 (1979): 133-41.

Lewis, Paula Gilbert. "The Themes of Memory and Death in Gabrielle Roy's *La Route d'Altamont.*" *Modern Fiction Studies* 22.3 (1976): 457-66.
Discusses *The Road Past Altamont.*

Lewis, Paula Gilbert. "Tragic and Humanistic Visions of the Future: The Fictional World of Gabrielle Roy." *Québec Studies* 1.1 (1983): 234-45.
Overview.

Lewis, Paula Gilbert. "Unsuccessful Couples, Shameful Sex, and Infrequent Love in the Fictional World of Gabrielle Roy." *Antigonish Review* 48 (1982): 49-55.
Overview.

Livesay, Dorothy. "Two Women Writers: Anglophone and Francophone." *Language and Literature in Multicultural Contexts*. Ed. Satendra Nandan. Suva, Fiji: University of the South Pacific, 1983. 234-39.
Discusses *Windflower* and *Children of My Heart.*

Lougheed, W. C. Introduction. *The Cashier*. By Gabrielle Roy. Trans. Harry Lorin Binsse. New Canadian Library 40. Toronto: McClelland and Stewart, 1963. vii-xiii.

Marshall, Joyce. "Gabrielle Roy 1909-1983." *Antigonish Review* 55 (1983): 35-46.
Overview.

Marshall, Joyce. "Gabrielle Roy, 1909-1983: Some Reminiscences." *Canadian Literature* 101 (1984): 183-84.
Overview.

Marshall, Joyce, trans. Introduction. *The Road Past Altamont*. By Gabrielle Roy. New Canadian Library 129. Toronto: McClelland and Stewart, 1966. vii-xi.

May, Cedric. *Breaking the Silence*: *The Literature of Québec*. Birmingham, Eng.: University of Birmingham, Regional Studies Centre, 1981. 91-94, 142-48.
Overview.

May, Cedric. "The Flickering Lights of Planet Earth: The Presentation of Manitoba in the Works of Gabrielle Roy." *Bulletin of Canadian Studies* 5.2 (1981): 38-47.
Overview.

McClelland, Jack. "Gabrielle Roy." *Quill and Quire* Sept. 1983: 60-61.
Obituary.

McClung, Molly G. *Women in Canadian Literature*. Toronto: Fitzhenry and Whiteside, 1977. 47-48, 54.
Overview.

McMullen, Lorraine. Introduction. *Windflower*. By Gabrielle Roy. Trans. Joyce Marshall. New Canadian Library 120. Toronto: McClelland and Stewart, 1975. n. pag.

McPherson, Hugo. "The Garden and the Cage: The Achievement of Gabrielle Roy." *Canadian Literature* 1 (1959): 46-57.
Overview.

McPherson, Hugo. Introduction. *The Tin Flute*. By Gabrielle Roy. Trans. Hannah Josephson. New Canadian Library 5. Toronto: McClelland and Stewart, 1958. v-xi.

Mead, Gerald. "The Representation of Solitude in *Bonheur d'occasion*." *Québec Studies* 7 (1988): 116-36.
Discusses *The Tin Flute*.

Mitcham, Allison. "Gabrielle Roy's Children." *Antigonish Review* 36 (1979): 95-99.
Discusses *The Tin Flute*, *Children of My Heart* and *Where Nests the Water Hen*.

Mitcham, Allison. "Imagination and the Capacity to Dream: A Study in Contemporary Canadian Fiction." *Revue de l'Université de Moncton* 6.3 (1973): 75-80.
Discusses *The Cashier*, *The Hidden Mountain* and *Windflower*.

Mitcham, Allison. *The Literary Achievement of Gabrielle Roy*. Fredericton, N.B.: York Press, 1983.
Overview.

Mitcham, Allison. *The Northern Imagination: A Study of Northern Canadian Literature*. Moonbeam, Ont.: Penumbra, 1983. passim.
Overview.

Mitcham, Allison. "The Northern Innocent in the Fiction of Gabrielle Roy." *Humanities Association Bulletin* 24.1 (1973): 25-31.
Overview.

Mitcham, Allison. "The Novelist as Reporter: Gabrielle Roy's *Fragiles lumières de la terre.*" *Dalhousie Review* 59.1 (1979): 180-83.
Discusses *The Fragile Lights of Earth.*

Mitcham, Allison. "Roy's West." *Canadian Literature* 88 (1981): 161-63.
Overview.

Moore, Brian. "The Woman on Horseback." *Great Canadians: A Century of Achievement*. Toronto: Canadian Centennial Library, 1965. 95-98.
Discusses *The Tin Flute.*

Murphy, John J. "*Alexandre Chenevert*: Gabrielle Roy's Crucified Canadian." *Queen's Quarterly* 72.2 (1965): 334-46.
Discusses *The Cashier.*

Murphy, John J. "Visit With Gabrielle Roy." *Thought* 38.148 (1963): 447-55.
Interview.

O'Donnell, Kathleen. "Gabrielle Roy's Portrait of the Artist." *Revue de l'Université d'Ottawa* 44.1 (1974): 70-77.
Discusses *Street of Riches* and *The Road Past Altamont.*

Randall, Julia. "Gabrielle Roy: Granddaughter of Quebec." *Hollins Critic* 14.5 (1977): 1-12.
Overview.

Roper, Gordon. Introduction. *Where Nests the Water Hen.* By Gabrielle Roy. Trans. Harry Lorin Binsse. New Canadian Library 25. Toronto: McClelland and Stewart, 1970. vi-x.

Ross, Malcolm. Introduction. *The Hidden Mountain.* By Gabrielle Roy. Trans. Harry Lorin Binsse. New Canadian Library 109. Toronto: McClelland and Stewart, 1975. n. pag.

Roy, Gabrielle. Interview. *New York Times Book Review* 1 June 1947: 8.

Roy, Gabrielle. "Saint-Henri Revisited." Trans. Jeanette Urbas and Lin Wilson. *Journal of Canadian Fiction* 24 (1979): 78-88.
Discusses *The Tin Flute.*

Shek, Ben-Zion. "*Bonheur d'occasion*, *Alexandre Chenevert*." *Social Realism in the French-Canadian Novel*. Montreal: Harvest House, 1977. 65-111, 153-56, 173-203.
Discusses *The Tin Flute* and *The Cashier*.

Shek, Ben-Zion. "The Jew in the French-Canadian Novel." *Viewpoints* 4.4 (1969): 29-35.
Discusses *The Cashier* and *The Tin Flute*.

Shek, Ben-Zion. "The Portrayal of Canada's Ethnic Groups in Some French-Canadian Novels." *Slavs in Canada: Proceedings of the Third National Conference on Canadian Slavs*. Ed. Cornelius E. Jaenen., Ottawa: Inter-University Committee on Canadian Slavs, 1970. 3: 269-80.
Overview.

Socken, Paul. "Art and the Artist in Gabrielle Roy's Works." *Revue de l'Université d'Ottawa* 45.3 (1975): 344-50.
Overview.

Socken, Paul. "Gabrielle Roy: An Annotated Bibliography." *The Annotated Bibliography of Canada's Major Authors*. Ed. Robert Lecker and Jack David. 7 vols to date. Downsview, Ont.: ECW Press, 1979-. 1: 213-63.

Socken, Paul. "Gabrielle Roy as Journalist." *Canadian Modern Language Review* 30.2 (1974): 96-100.
Discusses journalism and short stories published in journals.

Socken, Paul. "In Memoriam: Gabrielle Roy (1909-1983)." *Canadian Modern Language Review* 40.1 (1983): 105-10.
Obituary.

Socken, Paul. "'Le pays de l'amour' in the Works of Gabrielle Roy." *Revue de l'Université d'Ottawa* 46.3 (1976): 309-23.
Overview.

Socken, Paul. "Use of Language in *Bonheur d'occasion*: A Case in Point." *Essays on Canadian Writing* 11 (1978): 66-71.
Discusses *The Tin Flute*.

Socken, Paul Gerald. *The Influence of Physical and Social Environment of Character in the Novels of Gabrielle Roy*. Diss. University of Toronto, 1974.
Overview.

Stratford, Philip. Introduction. *The Tin Flute*. By Gabrielle Roy. Trans. Alan Brown. New Canadian Library 5. Toronto: McClelland and Stewart, 1982. n. pag.

Stratford, Philip. "Mainstream or Two Solitudes: Hugh MacLennan and Gabrielle Roy." *All the Polarities: Comparative Studies in Contemporary Canadian Novels in French and English*. Toronto: ECW Press, 1986. 12-29.
Discusses *The Tin Flute*.

Sutherland, Ronald. *Second Image: Comparative Studies in Quebec/Canadian Literature*. Toronto: New Press, 1971. 11-13.
Discusses *The Tin Flute*.

Sutherland, Ronald. "Twin Solitudes." *Canadian Literature* 31 (1967): 5-24.
Discusses *The Tin Flute*.

Thomas, A. Vernon. "The *Tin Flute* Turns Out to Be a Pot of Gold for Its Author." *Saturday Night* 12 Apr. 1947: 1+.

Thomas, Clara. "The Precious Kingdom: Fables of Our Literature." *Journal of Canadian Fiction* 1.2 (1972): 58-64.
Discusses *The Tin Flute*.

Thorne, W. B. "Poverty and Wrath: A Study of *The Tin Flute*." *Journal of Canadian Studies* 3.3 (1968): 3-10.

Tougas, Gérard. *History of French-Canadian Literature*. Trans. Alta Lind Cook. 2nd ed. Toronto: Ryerson Press, 1966. 151-55.
Overview.

Urbas, Jeanette. "Equations and Flutes." *Journal of Canadian Fiction* 1.2 (1972): 69-73.
Discusses *The Tin Flute*.

Urbas, Jeanette. "A Universal Theme." *From* Thirty Acres *to Modern Times: The Story of French-Canadian Literature*. Toronto: McGraw-Hill Ryerson, 1976. 45-63.
Overview.

van Lent, Peter. "Absence and Departure: The Male Mystique in French-Canadian Literature Before 1950." *American Review of Canadian Studies* 16.1 (1986): 17-23.
Discusses *The Tin Flute*.

Wagner, Janie. "*The Tin Flute*: A Note." *Canadian Literature* 70 (1976): 111-12.

Walker, E. A. "Gabrielle Roy." *Profiles in Canadian Literature*. Ed. Jeffrey M. Heath. Toronto: Dundurn Press, 1980. 1: 105-12.
Overview.

Warwick, Jack. *The Long Journey: Literary Themes of French Canada*. Toronto: University of Toronto Press, 1968. 86-100, 140-44.
Discusses *The Hidden Mountain* and *The Cashier*.

BOOK REVIEWS

THE CASHIER/ALEXANDRE CHENEVERT

Canadian Forum Apr. 1956: 20.
New York Times Book Review 16 Oct. 1955: 5.
Queen's Quarterly 63.1 (1956): 126-30.
Saturday Night 26 Nov. 1955: 18.
Saturday Review of Literature 31 Dec. 1955: 12.
University of Toronto Quarterly 24.3 (1955): 306-08.

CHILDREN OF MY HEART/CES ENFANTS DE MA VIE

Books in Canada May 1979: 17-18.
Branching Out 4.6 (1979): 37-39.
Canadian Book Review Annual (1980): 134.
Canadian Forum Aug. 1979: 29.
Canadian Literature 88 (1981): 124-26.
Chelsea Journal Sept.-Oct. 1979: 223-24.
Fiddlehead 122 (1979): 143-44.
Maclean's 12 Mar. 1979: 56.
Quarry 29.1 (1980): 92-96.
Quill and Quire Apr. 1979: 29.
Saturday Night May 1979: 50-52.
University of Toronto Quarterly 49.4 (1980): 390-91.

CLIPTAIL/COURTE-QUEUE

Canadian Book Review Annual (1980): 158.
Canadian Children's Literature 22 (1981): 45-46.

ENCHANTED SUMMER/CET ETE QUI CHANTAIT

Branching Out 4.4 (1977): 42-43.
Brick 3 (1978): 22.
Canadian Book Review Annual (1976): 155.
Journal of Canadian Fiction 2.2 (1973): 84-85.
Maclean's 20 Sept. 1976: 66.
Quill and Quire Nov. 1976: 32.

ENCHANTMENT AND SORROW/LA DETRESSE ET L'ENCHANTEMENT

American Review of Canadian Studies 15.2 (1985): 232-34.
Books in Canada Dec. 1987: 17-18.
Canadian Ethnic Studies 17.3 (1985): 160-62.
Canadian Literature 107 (1985): 129-30.
Maclean's 23 Nov. 1987: 54d+.
Quill and Quire Dec. 1987: 23.
University of Toronto Quarterly 58.1 (1988): 80-83.

THE FRAGILE LIGHTS OF EARTH/FRAGILES LUMIERES DE LA TERRE

Books in Canada June-July 1982: 19+.
Quill and Quire July 1982: 61.
University of Toronto Quarterly 52.4 (1983): 393.

GARDEN IN THE WIND/UN JARDIN AU BOUT DU MONDE ET AUTRES NOUVELLES

Books in Canada Nov. 1977: 34-35.
Branching Out 4.4 (1977): 42-43.
Canadian Author and Bookman 53.3 (1978): 35.
Canadian Book Review Annual (1977): 122.
Canadian Ethnic Studies 10.2 (1978): 201-02.
Canadian Forum Feb. 1978: 36.
Canadian Literature 82 (1979): 115-18.
Essays on Canadian Writing 9 (1977-78): 151-53.
Fiddlehead 122 (1979): 143-44.
Journal of Canadian Fiction 35-36 (1986): 172-74.
Quill and Quire 16 Sept. 1977: 8.
Saturday Night Nov. 1977: 69-72.
University of Toronto Quarterly 47.4 (1978): 388-89.

THE HIDDEN MOUNTAIN/LA MONTAGNE SECRETE

Canadian Author and Bookman 38.3 (1963): 10.
Canadian Literature 15 (1963): 74-76.
New York Times Book Review 28 Oct. 1962: 4+.
Renascence 16.1 (1963): 53-56.
Saturday Review of Literature 19 Jan. 1963: 44+.
Tamarack Review 27 (1963): 80-89.
University of Toronto Quarterly 32.4 (1963): 404.

THE ROAD PAST ALTAMONT/LA ROUTE D'ALTAMONT

Canadian Author and Bookman 42.4 (1967): 29.
Canadian Book Review Annual (1976): 139.
Canadian Literature 32 (1967): 59-60.
New York Times Book Review 11 Sept. 1966: 4-5.
Queen's Quarterly 74.3 (1967): 344-45.
Quill and Quire Apr. 1976: 40.
Saturday Review of Literature 3 Sept. 1966: 37.
Tamarack Review 42 (1967): 78-83.
University of Toronto Quarterly 36.4 (1967): 383.

STREET OF RICHES/RUE DESCHAMBAULT

Commonweal 25 Oct. 1957: 107-09.
New York Times Book Review 6 Oct. 1957: 4.
Queen's Quarterly 64.4 (1957-58): 627-29.
Saturday Night 9 Nov. 1957: 35-36.
Saturday Review of Literature 12 Oct. 1957: 55-56.
University of Toronto Quarterly 25.2 (1956): 394-95.

THE TIN FLUTE/BONHEUR D'OCCASION

Canadian Forum July 1947: 93-94.
Commonweal 23 May 1947: 147.
New York Times Book Review 20 Apr. 1947: 5.
New Yorker 26 Apr. 1947: 93-94.
Queen's Quarterly 54.2 (1947): 284-88.
Saturday Night 2 Mar. 1946: 17.
Saturday Review of Literature 24 May 1947: 12.
Times Literary Supplement 9 Oct. 1948: 565.
University of Toronto Quarterly 15.4 (1946): 412-13.
University of Toronto Quarterly 50.4 (1981): 92-95.

WHERE NESTS THE WATER HEN/LA PETITE POULE D'EAU

Canadian Forum Dec. 1951: 211-12.
Commonweal 26 Oct. 1951: 75-76.
New York Times Book Review 28 Oct. 1951: 32.
Saturday Night 3 Nov. 1951: 23.
Times Literary Supplement 5 Sept. 1952: 577.
University of Toronto Quarterly 20.4 (1951): 395-96.

WINDFLOWER/LA RIVIERE SANS REPOS

Branching Out 4.4 (1977): 43-44.
Canadian Literature 49 (1971): 83-85.
Maclean's Magazine Nov. 1970: 96.
Tamarack Review 57 (1971): 84-88.
University of Toronto Quarterly 40.4 (1971): 383.

SAVARD, FELIX-ANTOINE (1896-1982)

WORKS BY FELIX-ANTOINE SAVARD

Menaud, maître-draveur. Quebec: Garneau, 1937; rev. 1944; rev. Montreal: Fides, 1960, 1964. *Boss of the River.* Trans. Alan Sullivan. Toronto: Ryerson, 1947. *Master of the River.* Trans. Richard Howard. Montreal: Harvest House, 1976.

L'Abatis. Montreal: Fides, 1943; rev. 1960.

La Minuit. Montreal: Fides, 1948.

Le Barachois. Montreal: Fides, 1959.

Martin et le pauvre. Montreal: Fides, 1959.

La Folle. Montreal: Fides, 1960.

La Dalle-des-Morts. Montreal: Fides, 1965.

Symphonie du misereor. Ottawa: Editions de l'Université d'Ottawa, 1968.

Le Bouscueil. Montreal: Fides, 1972.

La Roche Ursule. Quebec: S. Allard, 1972.

Journal et souvenirs I: 1961-1962. Montreal: Fides, 1973.

Aux Marges du silence. Châteauguay, Que.: Michel Nantel, 1974; Quebec: Garneau, 1975.

Discours. Montreal: Fides, 1975.

Journal et souvenirs II: 1963-64. Montreal: Fides, 1975.

Discours d'un vieux sachem huron à l'occasion des fêtes du tricentenaire du diocèse de Québec. Lacolle, Que.: Michel Nantel, 1975.

Carnet du soir intérieur. Vol. One. Montreal: Fides, 1978.

Carnet du soir intérieur. Vol. Two. Montreal: Fides, 1979.

WORKS ABOUT FELIX-ANTOINE SAVARD

Cagnon, Maurice. *The French Novel of Quebec*. Boston: Twayne, 1986. 26-27.
Discusses *Boss of the River* and *La Minuit*.

Dorsinville, Max. *Caliban Without Prospero: Essay on Quebec and Black Literature*. Erin, Ont.: Porcépic, 1974. 59-75.
Discusses *Boss of the River*.

May, Cedric. *Breaking the Silence: The Literature of Québec*. Birmingham, Eng.: University of Birmingham, Regional Studies Centre, 1981. 87-90.
Discusses *Boss of the River*.

Runte, H. R. "Félix-Antoine Savard." *Canadian Writers, 1920-1959: First Series*. W. H. New. Dictionary of Literary Biography 68. Detroit: Gale, 1988. 324-27.
Overview.

Smith, Donald. "Félix-Antoine Savard: The Wonders of Nature." *Voices of Deliverance: Interviews with Quebec and Acadian Writers*. Trans. Larry Shouldice. Toronto: Anansi, 1986. 15-30.
Interview.

Tougas, Gérard. *History of French-Canadian Literature*. Trans. Alta Lind Cook. 2nd ed. Toronto: Ryerson Press, 1966. 164-68.
Overview.

Urbas, Jeanette. "The Myth of the Land." *From* Thirty Acres *to Modern Times: The Story of French-Canadian Literature*. Toronto: McGraw-Hill Ryerson, 1976. 13-18.
Discusses *Boss of the River*.

BOOK REVIEWS

L'ABATIS

University of Toronto Quarterly 13.4 (1944): 445.

BOSS OF THE RIVER/MASTER OF THE RIVER/MENAUD, MAITRE DRAVEUR

Canadian Book Review Annual (1976): 141.
Canadian Forum Nov. 1977: 39.
Dalhousie Review 27 (1947): 372-73.
Queen's Quarterly 54.2 (1947): 284-88.
University of Toronto Quarterly 7.4 (1938): 555-56.

THERIAULT, YVES (1915-1983)

WORKS BY YVES THERIAULT

Contes pour un homme seul. Montreal: Editions de l'Arbre, 1944.

La Fille laide. Montreal: Beauchemin, 1950.

Le Dompteur d'ours. Montreal: Cercle du Livre de France, 1951.

Les Vendeurs du temple. Quebec: Institut littéraire du Québec, 1951.

La Vengeance de la mer. Montreal: Publications du Lapin, 1951.

Aaron. Quebec: Institut littéraire du Québec, 1954.

Agaguk. Quebec: Institut littéraire du Québec, 1958. *Agaguk*. Trans. Miriam Chapin. Toronto: McGraw-Hill Ryerson Press, 1963.

Alerte au camp 29. Montreal: Beauchemin, 1959.

La Revanche du Nascopie. Montreal: Beauchemin, 1959.

Ashini. Montreal: Fides, 1960. *Ashini*. Trans. Gwendolyn Moore. Montreal: Harvest House, 1972.

La Loi de l'Apache. Montreal: Beauchemin, 1960.

Roi de la Côte Nord. Montreal: Editions de l'Homme, 1960.

Amour au goût de mer. Montreal: Beauchemin, 1961.

Les Commettants du Caridad. Quebec: Institut littéraire du Québec, 1961.

Cul-de-sac. Quebec: Institut littéraire du Québec, 1961. *Kesten and Cul-de-sac*. Trans. Gwendolyn Moore. Toronto: Clarke, Irwin and Co., 1973.

L'Homme de la Papinachois. Montreal: Beauchemin, 1961.

Séjour à Moscou. Montreal: Fides, 1961.

Le Vendeur d'étoiles, et autres contes. Montreal: Fides, 1961.

La Montagne sacrée. Montreal: Beauchemin, 1962.

Nakika, le petit Algonkin. Montreal: Leméac, 1962.

Le Rapt du Lac Caché. Montreal: Beauchemin, 1962.

Si la bombe m'était contée. Montreal: Editions du Jour, 1962.

Avea, le petit tramway. Montreal: Beauchemin, 1963.

Les Aventures de Ti-Jean. Montreal: Beauchemin, 1963.

Les Extravagances de Ti-Jean. Montreal: Beauchemin, 1963.

Le Grand Roman d'un petit homme. Montreal: Editions du Jour, 1963.

Maurice le Moruceau. Montreal: Beauchemin, 1963.

Nauya, le petit Esquimau. Montreal: Beauchemin, 1963.

Le Ru d'Ikoué. Montreal: Fides, 1963.

Ti-Jean et le Grand Géant. Montreal: Beauchemin, 1963.

La Rose de pierre; histoires d'amour. Montreal: Editions du Jour, 1964.

Zibon et Coucou. Montreal: Leméac, 1964.

La Montagne creuse. Montreal: Lidec, 1965.

Le Secret de Mufjarti. Montreal: Lidec, 1965.

Les Temps de carcajou. Quebec: Institut littéraire du Québec, 1965.

Le Château des petits hommes verts. Montreal: Lidec, 1966.

Les Dauphins de monsieur Yu. Montreal: Lidec, 1966.

Le Dernier Rayon. Montreal: Lidec, 1966.

L'Appelante. Montreal: Editions du Jour, 1967.

La Bête à 300 têtes. Montreal: Lidec, 1967.

Les Pieuvres. Montreal: Lidec, 1967.

Kesten. Montreal: Editions du Jour, 1968. *Kesten and Cul-de-sac.* Trans. Gwendolyn Moore. Toronto: Clarke, Irwin and Co., 1973.

L'île introuvable. Montreal: Editions du Jour, 1968.

Mahigan. Montreal: Leméac, 1968.

Le Marcheur. Montreal: Leméac, 1968.

La Mort d'eau. Montreal: Editions de l'Homme, 1968.

N'Tsuk. Montreal: Editions de l'Homme, 1968. *N'Tsuk.* Trans. Gwendolyn Moore. Montreal: Harvest House, 1972.

Les Vampires de la rue Monsieur-le-Prince. Montreal: Lidec, 1968.

Antoine et sa Montagne. Montreal: Editions du Jour, 1969.

L'Or de la felouque. Quebec: Editions Jeunesse, 1969.

Tayaout, fils d'Agaguk. Montreal: Editions de l'Homme, 1969.

Textes et documents. Montreal: Leméac, 1969.

Valérie. Montreal: Editions de l'Homme, 1969.

Le Dernier Havre. Montreal: L'Actuelle, 1970.

Frédange: pièce en deux actes suivi de Les Terres neuves, pièce en deux actes. Montreal: Leméac, 1970.

"Les Amours de Guillemette" in *Histoire de Lavaltrie en bref.* Ed. Jean C. Hétu. Lavaltrie: R. Pelletier, 1972.

La Passe-au-crachin. Montreal: Ferron Editeur, 1972.

Le Haut Pays. Montreal: Ferron Editeur, 1973.

Agoak: l'héritage d'Agaguk. Montreal: Stanké/Quinze, 1975. *Agoak: The Legacy of Agaguk.* Trans. John David Allan. Toronto: McGraw-Hill Ryerson, 1979.

Oeuvre de chair. Montreal: Stanké, 1975. *Ways of the Flesh*. Trans. Jean David. Agincourt, Ont.: Gage, 1977.

Moi, Pierre Huneau. Montreal: HMH, 1976.

Les Aventures d'Ori d'Or. Montreal: Editions Paulines, 1979.

Cajetan et la Taupe. Montreal: Editions Paulines, 1979.

Le Partage de minuit. Montreal: Québécor, 1980.

Popok, le petit Esquimau. Montreal: Québécor, 1980.

La Quête de l'ourse. Montreal: Stanké, 1980.

L'Etreinte de Vénus. Montreal: Québécor, 1981.

La Femme Anna et autres contes. Montreal: VLB Editeur, 1981.

Kuanuten (*Vent d'est*). Montreal: Editions Paulines, 1981.

Valère et le grand canot. Montreal: VLB Editeur, 1981.

L'Herbe de tendresse. Montreal: VLB, 1983.

WORKS ABOUT YVES THERIAULT

Aubrey, Irene E. "Yves Thériault." *Profiles*. Ed. Irma McDonough. Ottawa: Canadian Library Association, 1975. 145-48.
Biographical.

Bessette, Gérard. "French-Canadian Society as Seen by Contemporary Novelists." *Queen's Quarterly* 69.2 (1962): 177-97.
Overview.

Brazeau, J. Raymond. "Yves Thériault." *An Outline of Contemporary French Canadian Literature*. Toronto: Forum House, 1972. 21-28.
Discusses *Agaguk* and *Ashini*.

Cagnon, Maurice. *The French Novel of Quebec*. Boston: Twayne, 1986. 55-59.
Discusses *Aaron*, *Agaguk* and *Cul-de-sac*.

Cogswell, Fred. "The French Canadian Novel and the Problem of Social Change." *Journal of Canadian Fiction* 1.2 (1972): 65-68.
Discusses *Agaguk*.

Hesse, M. G. "An Interview with Yves Thériault." *Canadian Fiction Magazine* 47 (1983): 32-57.

Hesse, M. G. "The Significance of Death in the Work of Yves Thériault." *Journal of Canadian Fiction* 2.1 (1973): 43-48.
Overview.

May, Cedric. *Breaking the Silence: The Literature of Québec*. Birmingham, Eng.: University of Birmingham, Regional Studies Centre, 1981. 53-58.
Overview.

Mitcham, Allison. "The Canadian Matriarch: A Study in Contemporary French and English-Canadian Fiction." *Revue de l'Université de Moncton* 7.1 (1974): 37-42.
Discusses *Agaguk* and *Tayaout, fils d'Agaguk*.

Mitcham, Allison. "Flight: A Comparative Ecological Study Based on Contemporary French and English-Canadian Fiction." *Revue de l'Université de Moncton* 6.2 (1973): 86-105.
Overview.

Mitcham, Allison. "Imagination and the Capacity to Dream: A Study in Contemporary Canadian Fiction." *Revue de l'Université de Moncton* 6.3 (1973): 75-80.
Overview.

Mitcham, Allison. "The Isolation of Protesting Individuals Who Belong to Minority Groups (A Comparative Study in Contemporary Canadian Fiction)." *Wascana Review* 7.1 (1972): 43-50.
Overview.

Mitcham, Allison. *The Northern Imagination: A Study of Northern Canadian Literature*. Moonbeam, Ont.: Penumbra, 1983. passim.
Overview.

Mitcham, Allison. "Northern Mission Priest, Parson and Prophet in the North: A Study in French and English-Canadian Contemporary Fiction." *Laurentian University Review/Revue de l'Université Laurentienne* 7.1 (1974): 25-31.
Discusses *Ashini* and *Tayaout, fils d'Agaguk.*

Mitcham, Allison. "Yves Thériault: The Conscience of Contemporary Canada." *Laurentian University Review/Revue de l'Université Laurentienne* 5.1 (1972): 68-75.
Overview.

"News About People." *Saturday Night* 26 Apr. 1952: 36.
Biographical.

Shek, Ben-Zion. "The Jew in the French-Canadian Novel." *Viewpoints* 4.4 (1969): 29-35.
Discusses *Aaron.*

Shek, Ben-Zion. *Social Realism in the French-Canadian Novel.* Montreal: Harvest House, 1977. 157-69.
Discusses *Aaron.*

Smith, Donald. "Yves Thériault, Storyteller." *Voices of Deliverance: Interviews with Quebec and Acadian Writers.* Trans. Larry Shouldice. Toronto: Anansi, 1986. 57-81.
Interview.

Sutherland, Ronald. "The Body-Odeur of Race." *Canadian Literature* 37 (1968): 46-67.
Discusses *Aaron.*

Sutherland, Ronald. *Second Image: Comparative Studies in Quebec/Canadian Literature.* Toronto: New Press, 1971. 50-56.
Discusses *Aaron.*

Taaffe, Gerald. "Busy Individualist Behind an Exciting New Story." *Maclean's Magazine* 5 Oct. 1963: 80-81.
Discusses *Agaguk.*

Tougas, Gérard. *History of French-Canadian Literature.* Trans. Alta Lind Cook. 2nd ed. Toronto: Ryerson Press, 1966. 155-58.
Overview.

Urbas, Jeanette. "The Primitive Hero." *From* Thirty Acres to *Modern Times: The Story of French-Canadian Literature.* Toronto: McGraw-Hill Ryerson, 1976. 76-84.
Discusses *Agaguk* and *Ashini.*

Warwick, Jack. *The Long Journey: Literary Themes of French Canada.* Toronto: University of Toronto Press, 1968. 43-49, 64-68, 120-24.
Discusses *Agaguk*, *Ashini* and *Cul-de-sac.*

Warwick, Jack. "Yves Thériault and the Prix David." *Canadian Modern Language Review* 36.3 (1980): 383-91.
Overview.

Weiss, Jonathan. *French-Canadian Theater.* Boston: Twayne, 1986. 22-24.
Discusses *Le Marcheur.*

BOOK REVIEWS

AARON

University of Toronto Quarterly 24.3 (1955): 309-10.

AGAGUK

Canadian Author and Bookman 39.2 (1963): 15-16.
Canadian Forum Dec. 1963: 215.
Tamarack Review 31 (1964): 87-93.
Times Literary Supplement 17 Sept. 1964: 853.

AGOAK

Books in Canada May 1979: 15-16.
Canadian Book Review Annual (1979): 119-20.
Canadian Ethnic Studies 12.1 (1980): 123-24.
Maclean's 14 May 1979: 52.
Quill and Quire June 1979: 36-37.
University of Toronto Quarterly 49.4 (1980): 394-95.

ASHINI

Canadian Literature 10 (1961): 84-85.
Canadian Literature 59 (1974): 125-26.
University of Toronto Quarterly 42.4 (1973): 350.

CONTES POUR UN HOMME SEUL

University of Toronto Quarterly 14.3 (1945): 283.

CUL-DE-SAC

Canadian Literature 55 (1973): 114-15.

LE DERNIER HAVRE

Canadian Literature 55 (1973): 114-15.

LA FEMME ANNA ET AUTRES CONTES

French Review 56.4 (1983): 674-75.

LA FILLE LAIDE

University of Toronto Quarterly 20.4 (1951): 390-91.

N'TSUK

Canadian Literature 59 (1974): 125-26.
University of Toronto Quarterly 42.4 (1973): 350-51.

LA PARTAGE DE MINUIT

Canadian Literature 101 (1984): 117-19.

LES VENDEURS DU TEMPLE

University of Toronto Quarterly 21.4 (1952): 392-93.

WAYS OF THE FLESH/OEUVRE DE CHAIR

Canadian Book Review Annual (1977): 132.
Quill and Quire 9 July 1977: 4-5.

TREMBLAY, MICHEL (1942-)

WORKS BY MICHEL TREMBLAY

Contes pour buveurs attardés. Montreal: Editions du Jour, 1966. *Stories for Late Night Drinkers*. Trans. Michael Bullock. Vancouver: Intermedia, 1977.

Les Belles-Soeurs. Montreal: Holt, Rinehart and Winston, 1968. *Les Belles-Soeurs*. Trans. John Van Burek and Bill Glassco. Vancouver: Talonbooks, 1974.

La Cité dans l'oeuf. Montreal: Editions du Jour, 1969.

Lysistrata, d'après Aristophane. With André Brassard. Montreal: Leméac, 1969.

L'Effet des rayons gamma sur les vieux-garçons. Montreal: Leméac, 1970.

En pièces détachées; suivi de La Duchesse de Langeais. Montreal: Leméac, 1970. *Like Death Warmed Over* (*En pièces détachées*). Trans. Allan Van Meer. Toronto: Playwrights Co-op, 1973. *En pièces détachées*. Trans. Allan Van Meer. Vancouver: Talonbooks, 1975. *La Duchesse de Langeais and Other Plays*. Trans. John Van Burek. Vancouver: Talonbooks, 1976.

A toi, pour toujours, ta Marie-Lou. Montreal: Leméac, 1971. *Forever Yours, Marie-Lou*. Trans. John Van Burek and Bill Glassco. Vancouver: Talonbooks, 1975.

Trois petits tours. Montreal: Leméac, 1971. *La Duchesse de Langeais and Other Plays*. Trans. John Van Burek. Vancouver: Talonbooks, 1976.

Demain matin Montréal m'attend. Montreal: Leméac, 1972.

C't'à ton tour, Laura Cadieux. Montreal: Editions du Jour, 1973.

Hosanna, suivi de La Duchesse de Langeais. Montreal: Leméac, 1973. *Hosanna*. Trans. John Van Burek and Bill Glassco. Vancouver: Talonbooks, 1974.

Bonjour, là, bonjour. Montreal: Leméac, 1974. *Bonjour, là, bonjour*. Trans. John Van Burek and Bill Glassco. Vancouver: Talonbooks, 1975.

La Duchesse de Langeais and Other Plays. Trans. John Van Burek. Vancouver: Talonbooks, 1976.

Les Héros de mon enfance. Montreal: Leméac, 1976.

Sainte-Carmen de la Main. Montreal: Leméac, 1976. *Sainte-Carmen of the Main*. Trans. John Van Burek. Vancouver: Talonbooks, 1981.

Damnée Manon, sacrée Sandra, suivi de Surprise! Surprise! Montreal: Leméac, 1977. *Damnée Manon, sacrée Sandra*. Trans. John Van Burek. Vancouver: Talonbooks, 1981. *Surprise! Surprise!* translated in *La Duchesse de Langeais and Other Plays*. Trans. John Van Burek. Vancouver: Talonbooks, 1976.

La Grosse femme d'à côté est enceinte. Montreal: Leméac, 1978. *The Fat Woman Next Door is Pregnant*. Trans. Sheila Fischman. Vancouver: Talonbooks, 1981.

L'Impromptu d'Outremont. Montreal: Leméac, 1980. *The Impromptu of Outremont*. Trans. John Van Burek. Vancouver: Talonbooks, 1981.

Thérèse et Pierrette à l'école des Saints-Anges. Montreal: Leméac, 1980. *Therese and Pierrette and the Little Hanging Angel*. Trans. Sheila Fischman. Toronto: McClelland and Stewart, 1984.

Les Anciennes Odeurs. Montreal: Leméac, 1981. *Remember Me*. Trans. John Stowe. Vancouver: Talonbooks, 1984.

La Duchesse et le Roturier. Montreal: Leméac, 1982.

Oncle Vania. With Kim Yaroshevskaya. Montreal: Leméac, 1983.

Albertine, en cinq temps. Montreal: Leméac, 1984. *Albertine in Five Times*. Trans. John Van Burek and Bill Glassco. Vancouver: Talonbooks, 1986.

Des nouvelles d'Edouard. Montreal: Leméac, 1984.

Le Gars de Québec. Montreal: Leméac, 1985.

Le Coeur découvert: roman d'amours. Montreal: Leméac, 1986.

Six heures au plus tard. Montreal: Leméac, 1986.

Le Vrai monde? Montreal: Leméac, 1987. *The Real World?* Trans. John Van Burek and Bill Glassco. Vancouver: Talonbooks, 1988.

WORKS ABOUT MICHEL TREMBLAY

Ackerman, Marianne. "Sweet Jesus! Who's That Ma? It's Michel Tremblay - The Man Who Brought Gutter Talk to the Quebec Stage..." *Saturday Night* June 1988: 40-45+. General.

Anthony, Geraldine, ed. "Michel Tremblay." *Stage Voices: Twelve Canadian Playwrights Talk About Their Lives and Work.* Toronto: Doubleday, 1978. 275-90. Interview.

Antosh, R. B. "Michel Tremblay and the Fantastic of Violence." *Aspects of Fantasy: Selected Essays from the Second International Conference on the Fantastic in Literature and Film.* Ed. William Coyle. New York: Greenwood Press, 1986. 17-22. Discusses *Stories for Late Night Drinkers.*

Antosh, Ruth B. "Waiting for Prince Charming: Revisions and Deformations of the Cinderella Motif in Contemporary Quebec Theater." *Québec Studies* 6 (1988): 104-11. Discusses *Hosanna.*

Babby, Ellen Reisman. "*Des nouvelles d'Edouard*: Michel Tremblay's Fugal Composition." *American Review of Canadian Studies* 17.4 (1987-88): 383-94.

Collet, Paulette. "Fennario's *Balconville* and Tremblay's *En pièces détachées*: A Universe of Backyards and Despair." *Canadian Drama/L'art dramatique canadien* 10.1 (1984): 35-43. Discusses *Like Death Warmed Over.*

Czarnecki, Mark. "Five Prisoners of Guilt." Rev. of *Albertine in Five Times* by Michel Tremblay. *Maclean's* 22 Apr. 1985: 73.

Dorsinville, Max. "The Changing Landscape of Drama in Quebec." *Dramatists in Canada: Selected Essays*. Ed. William H. New. Vancouver: University of British Columbia Press, 1972. 179-95.
Overview.

Dostie, Bruno. "Michel Tremblay: Quebec's Superstar Playwright-Songwriter." *Canadian Composer* June 1977: 16-23.
Interview.

Dumas, Carmel. "Tremblay's Main is a Moveable Feast." *Quill and Quire* Nov. 1979: 15.
Overview.

Findlay, William. "*Les Belles Soeurs* (an extract): Michel Tremblay." *Cencrastus* 3 (1980): 4-8.

Forsyth, Louise. "First Person Feminine Singular: Monologues by Women in Several Modern Quebec Plays." *Canadian Drama/L'art dramatique canadien* 5.2 (1979): 189-203.
Overview.

Francoeur, Louis. "Quebec Theatre: Stimulation or Communication." *Contemporary Quebec Criticism*. Ed. and trans. Larry Shouldice. Toronto: University of Toronto Press, 1979. 171-94.
Discusses *Les Belles-Soeurs.*

Garebian, Keith. "Festival Lennoxville: Trash, Tinsel and Two Jewels." Rev. of *Hosanna* by Michel Tremblay. *Performing Arts in Canada* 15.3 (1978): 33-36.

Gerson, Mark. "The Indelible Mark of Tremblay's Theatre." *Performing Arts in Canada* 18.3 (1981): 25-27.
Interview.

Gobin, Pierre. "Michel Tremblay: An Interweave of Prose and Drama." Trans. Richard Deshaies. *Yale French Studies* 65 (1983): 106-23.
Overview.

Hopkins, Elaine R. "Michel Tremblay's *L'Impromptu d'Outremont*: Meaning and Mise en scène." *Québec Studies* 1.1 (1983): 191-97.
Discusses *The Impromptu of Outremont.*

Hunn, Robert C. "Michel Tremblay's *Hosanna* and Pirandello's 'teatro dello speccio.'" *Canadian Drama/L'art dramatique canadien* 6.2 (1980): 201-12.

King, Deirdre. "*L'Impromptu d'Outremont.*" *Canadian Forum* Dec. 1981-Jan. 1982: 44-45.
Discusses *The Impromptu of Outremont.*

Knelman, Martin. "Playwrights as Star of the Play." *Saturday Night* Apr. 1978: 59-60+.
Discusses *Sainte-Carmen of the Main.*

Knelman, Martin. "Tremblay's the Thing." *Toronto Life* Apr. 1986: 18.
Discusses *Albertine in Five Times.*

Kucherawy, Dennis. "Michel Tremblay: Dry Rot at the Grass Roots." *Performing Arts in Canada* 14.1 (1977): 44-45.
General.

Manguel, Alberto. "No Exit: In Michel Tremblay's Fiction, Quebec is a Prison in Which the Wardens are the Inmates Themselves." *Saturday Night* July 1984: 43-44+.
Discusses *Therese and Pierrette and the Little Hanging Angel.*

May, Cedric. *Breaking the Silence: The Literature of Québec.* Birmingham, Eng.: University of Birmingham, Regional Studies Centre, 1981. 165-70.
Discusses *C't'à ton tour, Laura Cadieux.*

McCarthy, Gerry. "Michel Tremblay." *Bulletin of Canadian Studies* 6.1 (1982): 54-64.
Overview.

McCaughna, David. "Michel Tremblay: No Longer 'That Nasty Boy From Quebec.'" *Scene Changes* Feb.-Mar. 1975: 9-10.
Interview.

McQuaid, Catherine. "Michel Tremblay's Seduction of the Other Solitude." *Canadian Drama/L'art dramatique canadien* 2.2 (1976): 219-23.
Overview.

"Michel Tremblay Winds Up *Belles soeurs* Cycle, Collaborates with Brassard on New Film Smash." *Canadian Composer* Apr. 1977: 42.
General.

Nardocchio, Elaine. "Structural Analysis of Drama: Practical and Theoretical Implications." *Computers and the Humanities* 19.4 (1985): 221-23.
Discusses *Les Belles-Soeurs.*

Nardocchio, Elaine F. "Structural Analysis of Drama: A Québécois Example." *Computers in Literary and Linguistic Computing: Proceedings of the Eleventh International Conference.* Paris: Champion-Slatkine, 1985. 267-75.
Discusses *Les Belles-Soeurs.*

Nardocchio, Elaine F. *Theatre and Politics in Modern Quebec.* Edmonton: University of Alberta Press, 1986. 66-73.
Overview.

Pagé, Raymond. "Theatre in Quebec." *Chelsea Journal* Mar.-Apr. 1975: 85-94.
Discusses *Les Belles-Soeurs* and *Forever Yours, Marie-Lou.*

Parker, Brian. "Is There a Canadian Drama?" *The Canadian Imagination: Dimensions of a Literary Culture.* Ed. David Staines. Cambridge, MA: Harvard University Press, 1977. 152-87.
Discusses *Forever Yours, Marie-Lou.*

Parris, David L. "Cats in the Literature of Quebec." *British Journal of Canadian Studies* 3.2 (1988): 259-66.
Discusses *The Fat Woman Next Door is Pregnant, Therese and Pierrette and the Little Hanging Angel* and *La Duchesse et le roturier.*

"Peering Into the Soul of French Canada (Michel Tremblay)." *Maclean's* 13 Apr. 1987: 46.
General.

Quig, James. "The Joual Revolution." *Canadian Magazine* 14 May, 1977: 16-19.
General.

Ripley, John. "From Alienation to Transcendence: The Quest for Selfhood in Michel Tremblay's Plays." *Canadian Literature* 85 (1980): 44-59.
Overview.

Rubin, Don. "Michel Tremblay Casebook: Introduction." *Canadian Theatre Review* 24 (1979): 11.
General.

Rubin, Don, and John Van Burek. "Tremblay in Translation." *Canadian Theatre Review* 24 (1979): 42-46.
Interview.

Rudakoff, Judith. "Michel Tremblay." *Profiles in Canadian Literature*. Ed. Jeffrey M. Heath. Toronto: Dundurn Press, 1986. 6: 65-72.
Overview.

Russell, Delbert W. "Biographical Checklist: Michel Tremblay." *Canadian Theatre Review* 24 (1979): 47-51.

Serafin, Bruce. "Five Short Plays by Tremblay." *Essays on Canadian Writing* 11 (1978): 248-59.
Discusses *La Duchesse de Langeais and Other Plays.*

Shek, Ben. "Quebec: French Canadian Playwright Michel Tremblay." *Performing Arts in Canada* 8.3 (1971): 28-29.
Interview.

Smith, Donald. "Michel Tremblay and the Collective Memory." *Voices of Deliverance: Interviews with Quebec and Acadian Writers*. Trans. Larry Shouldice. Toronto: Anansi, 1986. 205-41.
Interview.

Twigg, Alan. "Michel Tremblay: Quebec." *For Openers: Conversations with 24 Canadian Writers*. Madeira Park, B.C.: Harbour Publishing, 1981. 151-61.
Interview.

Usmiani, Renate, and André Brassard. "Discovering the Nuances." *Canadian Theatre Review* 24 (1979): 38-41.
Interview with Brassard regarding the staging of Tremblay's plays.

Usmiani, Renate. "Hyperrealism: Michel Tremblay and Franz Xaver Kroets." *Canadian Drama/L'art dramatique canadien* 13.2 (1987): 201-09.
Overview.

Usmiani, Renate. "Michel Tremblay." *Canadian Writers Since 1960: Second Series*. Ed. W. H. New. Dictionary of Literary Biography 60. Detroit: Gale, 1987. 342-52.
Overview.

Usmiani, Renate. *Michel Tremblay: A Critical Study*. Vancouver: Douglas and McIntyre, 1982.
Overview.

Usmiani, Renate. "Michel Tremblay's *Sainte Carmen*: Synthesis and Orchestration." *Canadian Drama/L'art dramatique canadien* 2.2 (1976): 206-18.
Discusses *Sainte-Carmen of the Main*.

Usmiani, Renate. "The Musical Comedies of Michel Tremblay: Lighter Side of Alienation and Identity Crisis." *Canadian Drama/L'art dramatique canadien* 6.2 (1980): 192-200.
Discusses *Demain matin Montréal m'attend* and *Les Héros de mon enfance*.

Usmiani, Renate. "The Tremblay Opus: Unity in Diversity." *Canadian Theatre Review* 24 (1979): 12-25.
Overview.

Usmiani, Renate. "Where to Begin the Accusation." *Canadian Theatre Review* 24 (1979): 26-37.
Interview.

Wallace, Robert. "Tales of Two Cities: Interview with Maurice Podbrey." *Canadian Theatre Review* 46 (1986): 6-13.
Discusses staging of *Albertine in Five Times*.

Weinstein, Ann. "Some Thoughts on Tremblay at Lennoxville: Scenes from a Working-Class Marriage." *Canadian Drama/L'art dramatique canadien* 3.2 (1977): 227-29.
Discusses *Forever Yours, Marie-Lou*.

Weiss, Jonathan. "Toward a New Realism: Michel Tremblay." *French-Canadian Theater*. Boston: Twayne, 1986. 22-24, 24-48.
Overview.

Weiss, Jonathan M. "The Contemporary Theatre and Its Public in Quebec." *Québec Studies* 1.1 (1983): 166-77. Overview.

Wilson, Neil. "Michel Tremblay: A Profile of a Successful Playwright." *Performing Arts in Canada* 23.1 (1986): 28-29. Discusses *Albertine in Five Times.*

BOOK REVIEWS

ALBERTINE IN FIVE TIMES/ALBERTINE, EN CINQ TEMPS

Books in Canada May 1987: 22.
Canadian Book Review Annual (1987): 199.
Queen's Quarterly 95.4 (1988): 967-68.
Quill and Quire June 1987: 31.
University of Toronto Quarterly 57.1 (1987): 87-88.

LES BELLES SOEURS

Books in Canada June 1975: 24-26.
Brick 3 (1978): 5-6.
Canadian Literature 66 (1975): 112-16.
Canadian Theatre Review 9 (1976): 181-82.
Quarry 25.1 (1976): 77-79.
Queen's Quarterly 86.2 (1979): 365-66.
Quill and Quire Apr. 1975: 36.
Tamarack Review 68 (1976): 86-89.

BONJOUR, LA, BONJOUR

Books in Canada Apr. 1977: 14-15.
Canadian Book Review Annual (1976): 209.
Quill and Quire Aug. 1976: 40.

LE COEUR DECOUVERT

Books in Canada Apr. 1987: 31-32.

DAMNEE MANON, SACREE SANDRA

Books in Canada Apr. 1982: 9.
Canadian Book Review Annual (1981): 195.
Canadian Literature 98 (1983): 76-79.
Quarry 31.3 (1982): 111-15.
University of Toronto Quarterly 51.4 (1982): 396-98.

DAMNEE MANON, SACREE SANDRA, SUIVI DE SURPRISE! SURPRISE!

Canadian Theatre Review 15 (1977): 159-60.

LA DUCHESSE DE LANGEAIS AND OTHER PLAYS

Canadian Book Review Annual (1976): 219.
Canadian Literature 76 (1978): 101-04.
Quill and Quire June 1977: 44.
University of Toronto Quarterly 47.4 (1978): 391-93.

LA DUCHESSE ET LE ROTURIER

French Review 57.1 (1983): 143-44.

THE FAT WOMAN NEXT DOOR IS PREGNANT/LA GROSSE FEMME D'A COTE EST ENCEINTE

Books in Canada Feb. 1982: 28.
Canadian Book Review Annual (1982): 155.
Canadian Literature 98 (1983): 76-79.
Maclean's 2 Apr. 1977: 42+.
Performing Arts in Canada 16.1 (1979): 52.
Quill and Quire Feb. 1982: 38.
University of Toronto Quarterly 51.4 (1982): 395-96.

FOREVER YOURS, MARIE-LOU/A TOI, POUR TOUJOURS, TA MARIE-LOU

Books in Canada June 1975: 24-26.
Brick 3 (1978): 5-6.
Matrix 1.1 (1975): 28-29.
Queen's Quarterly 86.2 (1979): 365-66.
Quill and Quire Oct. 1975: 14.
University of Toronto Quarterly 45.4 (1976): 364-65.

HOSANNA

Books in Canada June 1975: 24-26.
Brick 3 (1978): 5-6.
Canadian Literature 66 (1975): 112-16.
Matrix 1.1 (1975): 28-29.
Quill and Quire Mar. 1975: 20.
Tamarack Review 66 (1975): 105-06.
University of Toronto Quarterly 44.4 (1975): 354.

THE IMPROMPTU OF OUTREMONT/L'IMPROMPTU D'OUTREMONT

Books in Canada Apr. 1982: 9.
Canadian Book Review Annual (1981): 195.
Canadian Literature 98 (1983): 76-79.
Quarry 31.3 (1982): 111-15.
Quill and Quire Apr. 1982: 29.
University of Toronto Quarterly 51.4 (1982): 396-98.

LIKE DEATH WARMED OVER/EN PIECES DETACHEES

Canadian Book Review Annual (1975): 152.
University of Toronto Quarterly 45.4 (1976): 363.

ONCLE VANIA

Canadian Literature 102 (1984): 171-74.

REMEMBER ME/LES ANCIENNES ODEURS

Books in Canada Jan.-Feb. 1986: 20-21.
Canadian Book Review Annual (1984): 284.
Canadian Literature 98 (1983): 76-79.
Canadian Literature 112 (1987): 180-83.
French Review 56.5 (1983): 796-97.
University of Toronto Quarterly 56.1 (1986): 81.

SAINTE-CARMEN OF THE MAIN/SAINTE-CARMEN DE LA MAIN

Books in Canada Apr. 1982: 9.
Canadian Book Review Annual (1981): 196.
Canadian Literature 98 (1983): 76-79.
Canadian Theatre Review 15 (1977): 159-60.
Quarry 31.3 (1982): 111-15.
Quill and Quire Apr. 1982: 29.
University of Toronto Quarterly 51.4 (1982): 396-98.

STORIES FOR LATE NIGHT DRINKERS/CONTES POUR BUVEURS ATTARDES

Books in Canada Nov. 1978: 16-17.
Brick 10 (1980): 9.
Canadian Book Review Annual (1979): 165-66.
Canadian Forum Jan.-Feb. 1979: 40-42.
Matrix 8 (1979): 68.
Quill and Quire 8 Sept. 1978: 10-11.

THERESE AND PIERRETTE AND THE LITTLE HANGING ANGEL/THERESE ET PIERRETTE A L'ECOLE DES SAINTS-ANGES

Books in Canada Jan.-Feb. 1985: 32-33+.
Canadian Book Review Annual (1984): 203.
Canadian Literature 88 (1981): 118-19.
Canadian Literature 103 (1984): 123-25.
French Review 55.3 (1982): 444-45.
Maclean's 30 Apr. 1984: 57+.
Matrix 19 (1984): 72-73.
Quill and Quire June 1984: 30.
University of Toronto Quarterly 54.4 (1985): 391.

INDEX TO CRITICS

* indicates two or more references

* indicates two or more references

* indicates two or more references

* indicates two or more references

* indicates two or more references

* indicates two or more references

* indicates two or more references

* indicates two or more references

* indicates two or more references

INDEX TO EDITORS

* indicates two or more references

* indicates two or more references

CANADIAN PUBLISHERS' ADDRESSES

PERIODICALS

Acadiensis
University of New Brunswick,
Department of History,
Fredericton, N.B.
E3B 5A3

Antigonish Review
St. Francis Xavier University,
Antigonish, N.S.
B2G 1CO

ArtsAtlantic
Confederation Centre Art Gallery and Museum,
Box 848,
Charlottetown, P.E.I.
C1A 7L9

Atkinson Review of Canadian Studies
Atkinson College,
York University,
4700 Keele St.,
North York, Ont.
M3J 1P3

Atlantic Advocate
University of New Brunswick Press,
Box 3370,
Fredericton, N.B.
E3B 5A2

Atlantic Insight
Insight Publishing Ltd.,
1668 Barrington St.,
Halifax, N.S.
B3J 2A2

Atlantis: A Women's Studies Journal
Mount Saint Vincent University,
166 Bedford Hwy,
Halifax, N.S.
B3M 2J6

Books in Canada
Canadian Review of Books Ltd.,
366 Adelaide St. E.,
Toronto, Ont.
M5A 3X9

Brick: A Journal of Reviews
Brick Books,
P.O. Box 537,
Station Q,
Toronto, Ont.
M4T 2M5

Broadside: A Feminist Review
Broadside Review,
Box 494,
Station P,
Toronto, Ont.
M5S 2T1

CV2
Territories Publishing Corporation,
Box 32,
University Centre,
University of Manitoba,
Winnipeg, Man.
R3T 1EO

Canadian Author and Bookman
Canadian Authors Association,
121 Avenue Rd.,
Suite 104,
Toronto, Ont.
M5R 2G3

Canadian Book Review Annual
Simon & Pierre Publishing Co. Ltd.,
P.O. Box 280,
Adelaide St. Station,
Toronto, Ont.
M5C 2J4

Canadian Business
CB Media,
70 The Esplanade,
2nd Floor,
Toronto, Ont.
M5E 1R2

Canadian Children's Literature
Canadian Children's Press,
University of Guelph,
Dept. of English,
Guelph, Ont.
N1G 2W1

Canadian Composer
Composers Authors and Publishers Association of Canada,
Creative Arts Co.,
1240 Bay St.,
Suite 303,
Toronto, Ont.
M5R 2A7

Canadian Drama/L'art dramatique canadien
University of Guelph,
Department of English,
Guelph, Ont.
N1G 2W1

Canadian Ethnic Studies
Canadian Ethnic Studies Association,
Dalhousie University,
Dept. of Sociology,
Halifax, N.S.
B3H 1T2

Canadian Fiction Magazine
Geoffrey Hancock,
Box 946,
Station F,
Toronto, Ont.
M4Y 2N9

Canadian Forum
Survival Foundation,
70 The Esplanade,
3rd Floor,
Toronto, Ont.
M5E 1R2

Canadian Literature
University of British Columbia,
223-2029 West Mall,
Vancouver, B.C.
V6T 1W5

Canadian Modern Language Review
237 Hellems Ave.,
Welland, Ont.
L3B 3B8

Canadian Review of Comparative Literature
Canadian Comparative Literature Association,
Academic Printing and Publishing,
Box 4834,
Edmonton, Alta.
T6E 5G7

Canadian Theatre Review
University of Toronto Press,
5201 Dufferin St.,
North York, Ont.
M3H 5T8

Canadian Woman Studies/Cahiers de la femme
York University,
Inanna Publications and Education Inc.,
212 Founders College,
4700 Keele St.,
North York, Ont.
M3J 1P3

Canadian Women's Studies see *Canadian Woman Studies*

Chatelaine
Maclean Hunter Ltd.,
Magazine Division,
Maclean-Hunter Bldg.,
777 Bay St.,
Toronto, Ont.
M5W 1A7

Contemporary Verse 2 see *CV2*

Cross-Canada Writers' Magazine
Cross-Canada Writers, Inc.,
P.O. Box 277,
Station F,
Toronto, Ont.
M4Y 2L7

Cross-Canada Writers' Quarterly see *Cross-Canada Writers' Magazine*

Dalhousie French Studies
Dalhousie University,
Dept. of French,
Halifax, N.S.
B3H 3J5

Dalhousie Review
Dalhousie University Press,
Sir James Dunn Bldg.,
Suite 314,
Halifax, N.S.
B3H 3J5

Ellipse
Université de Sherbrooke,
Faculté des Lettres et Sciences Humaines,
Box 10,
Sherbrooke, Que.
J1K 2R1

Essays on Canadian Writing
Canadian Literary Research Foundation,
307 Coxwell Ave.,
Toronto, Ont.
M4L 3B5

Event
Douglas College,
Box 2503,
New Westminster, B.C.
V3L 5B2

Exile
Exile Editions Ltd.,
69 Sullivan St.,
Toronto, Ont.
M5T 1C2

Fiddlehead
University of New Brunswick,
Old Arts Building,
Rm. 317,
P.O. Box 4400,
Fredericton, N.B.
E3B 5A3

Financial Post
Financial Post,
777 Bay St.,
Toronto, Ont.
M5G 2E4

Fireweed: A Feminist Quarterly
Fireweed Inc.,
Box 279,
Station B,
Toronto, Ont.
M5T 2W2

Forces
Societé d'édition de la revue Forces,
500 Rue Sherbrooke W.,
Bureau 430,
Montreal, Que.
H3A 3C6

Idler
M. Drucker,
P.O. Box 280,
Station E,
Toronto, Ont.
M6H 4E2

International Fiction Review
International Fiction Association,
Dept. of German and Russian,
University of New Brunswick,
Fredericton, N.B.
E3B 5A3

Journal of Canadian Fiction
Journal of Canadian Fiction Press Association,
2050 Mackay St.,
Montreal, Que.
H3G 2J1

Journal of Canadian Studies
Trent University,
Peterborough, Ont.
K9J 7B8

Literature and Ideology see *New Literature and Ideology*

New Literature and Ideology
Canadian Cultural Workers Committee,
Box 727,
Adelaide Station,
Toronto, Ont.
M5C 2J8

Maclean's
Maclean Hunter Ltd.,
Magazine Division,
Maclean-Hunter Bldg.,
777 Bay St.,
Toronto, Ont.
M5W 1A7

Malahat Review
University of Victoria,
Box 1700,
Victoria, B.C.
V8W 2Y2

Matrix
Linda Leith,
P.O. Box 100,
Ste-Anne-de-Bellevue, Que.
H9X 3L3

Meta
Presses de l'Université de Montréal,
C.P. 6128,
Succ. A,
Montreal, Que.
H3C 3J7

Modern Drama
University of Toronto,
Graduate Centre for the Study of Drama,
University of Toronto Press,
Journals Dept.,
63A St. George St.,
Toronto, Ont.
M5S 1A6

Mosaic
University of Manitoba,
208 Tier Bldg.,
Winnipeg, Man.
R3T 2N2

Open Letter
Frank Davey,
104 Lyndhurst Ave.,
Toronto, Ont.
M5R 2Z7

Papers of the Bibliographical Society of Canada
/Cahiers de la société bibliographique du Canada
Bibliographical Society of Canada,
P.O. Box 575,
Station P,
Toronto, Ont.
M5S 2T1

Performing Arts in Canada
Canadian Stage & Arts Publications, Ltd.,
263 Adelaide St. W.,
Toronto, Ont.
M5H 1Y2

Poetry Canada Review
Canadian Literary Research Foundation,
307 Coxwell Ave.,
Toronto, Ont.
M4L 3B5

Prism International
University of British Columbia,
Creative Writing Department,
E462-1866 Main Mall,
Vancouver, B.C.
V6T 1W5

Quarry
Quarry Press, Inc.,
Box 1061,
Kingston, Ont.
K7L 4Y5

Queen's Quarterly
Queen's University,
Kingston, Ont.
K7L 3N6

Quill and Quire
Key Publishers Co. Ltd.,
56 The Esplanade,
Suite 213,
Toronto, Ont.
M5E 1A7

Resources for Feminist Research/Documentation sur la recherche feministe
Ontario Institute for Studies in Education,
252 Bloor St. W.,
Toronto, Ont.
M5S 1V6

Revue de l'Université d'Ottawa
University of Ottawa Press,
603 Cumberland,
Ottawa, Ont.
K1N 6N5

Revue de l'Université de Moncton
Université de Moncton,
Moncton, N.B.
E1A 3E9

Revue de l'Université Sainte-Anne
Université Sainte-Anne,
Church Point, N.S.
B0W 1M0

Room of One's Own
Growing Room Collective,
Box 46160,
Station G,
Vancouver, B.C.
V6R 4G5

Royal Society of Canada. Transactions
Royal Society of Canada,
344 Wellington St.,
Ottawa, Ont.
K1A 0N4

Rubicon
McGill University,
853 rue Sherbrooke St. W.,
Montreal, Que.
H3A 2T6

Saturday Night
Saturday Night Publishing Services,
511 King St. W.,
Suite 100,
Toronto, Ont.
M5V 2Z4

Sphinx
University of Regina.
Dept. of English,
Regina, Sask.
S4S 0A2

Spirale
C.P. 98,
Succ. E,
Montreal, Que.
H2T 3A5

Studies in Canadian Literature
University of New Brunswick,
Dept. of English,
Fredericton, N.B.
E3B 5A3

Thalia
Association for the Study of Humor,
c/o Jacqueline Tavernier-Courbin, Ed.,
Dept. of English,
University of Ottawa,
Ottawa, Ont.
K1N 6N5

Toronto Life
Toronto Life Publishing Co. Ltd.,
59 Front St. E.,
Toronto, Ont.
M5E 1B3

University of Toronto Quarterly
University of Toronto Press,
Journals Dept.
63A St. George St.,
Toronto, Ont.
M5S 1A6

University of Windsor Review
University of Windsor,
Windsor, Ont.
N9B 3P4

Viewpoints (supplement to *Canadian Jewish News*)
Labor Zionist Movement of Canada,
c/o Canadian Jewish Congress,
1590 Avenue Docteur Penfield,
Montreal, Que.
H3G 1C5

West Coast Review
Simon Fraser University,
West Coast Review Publishing Society,
Burnaby, B.C.
V5A 1S6

MONOGRAPHS (ENGLISH LANGUAGE)

Anansi see House of Anansi Press

Borealis Press Ltd.
9 Ashburn Dr.,
Ottawa, Ont.
K2E 6N4

Coach House Press
401 (rear) Huron St.,
Toronto, Ont.
M5S 2G5

Doubleday Canada Ltd.
105 Bond St.,
Toronto, Ont.
M5B 1Y3

Douglas and McIntyre
1615 Venables St.,
Vancouver, B.C.
V5L 2H1

Dundurn Press Ltd.
2181 Queen St. E.,
Suite 301,
Toronto, Ont.
M4E 1E5

ECW Press
307 Coxwell Ave.,
Toronto, Ont.
M4L 3B5
Order from: University of Toronto Press

Eden Press Inc.
31A Westminster Ave.,
Montreal, Que.
H4X 1Y8

Exile Editions Ltd.
69 Sullivan St.,
Toronto, Ont.
M5T 1C2
Order from: General Publishing Co. Ltd.

Fitzhenry & Whiteside Ltd.
195 Allstate Parkway,
Markham, Ont.
L3R 4T8

Gage Educational Publishing
164 Commander Blvd.,
Agincourt, Ont.
M1S 3C7

General Publishing Co. Ltd.
30 Lesmill Rd.,
Don Mills, Ont.
M3B 2T6

Guernica Editions Inc.
P.O. Box 633,
Station N.D.G.,
Montreal, Que.
H4A 3R1

Harbour Publishing Co. Ltd.
P.O. Box 219,
Madeira Park, B.C.
V0N 2H0

Harvest House Ltd. Publishers
1200 Atwater Ave.,
Suite 1,
Montreal, Que.
H32 1X4

Les Editions Héritage Inc.
300 ave. Arran,
St-Lambert, Que.
J4R 1K5

House of Anansi Press
35 Britain St.,
Toronto, Ont.
M5A 1R7
Order from: University of Toronto Press

Editions Hurtubise HMH Ltée
7360, boul. Newman,
Ville LaSalle, Que.
H8N 1X2

Lester & Orpen Dennys Ltd., Publishers
78 Sullivan St.,
Toronto, Ont.
M5T 1C1
Order from: University of Toronto Press

Macmillan of Canada
29 Birch Ave.,
Toronto, Ont.
M4V 1E2

McClelland and Stewart
481 University Ave.,
Suite 900,
Toronto, Ont.
M5G 2E9
Distribution Centre:
25 Hollinger Rd.,
Toronto, Ont.
M4B 3G2

McGraw-Hill Ryerson Ltd.
330 Progress Ave.,
Scarborough, Ont.
M1P 2Z5

Musson Publishing
30 Lesmill Rd.,
Don Mills, Ont.
M3B 2TC

NeWest Publishers Ltd.,
310, 10359-82 Ave.,
Edmonton, Alta.
T6E 1Z4

Oberon Press
400 - 350 Sparks St.,
Ottawa, Ont.
K1R 7S8

Oxford University Press
70 Wynford Dr.,
Don Mills, Ont.
M3C 1J9

Penumbra Press
P.O. Box 248,
Kapuskasing, Ont.
P5N 2Y4
Order from: University of Toronto Press

Playwrights Union of Canada
54 Wolseley St.,
2nd Floor,
Toronto, Ont.
M5T 1A5

Porcépic Books
4252 Commerce Crt.,
Victoria, B.C.
V82 4M2

Les Editions de la Presse
44 ouest, rue St-Antoine,
Montreal, Que.
H2Y 1J5

Simon & Pierre Publishing Co. Ltd.
P.O. Box 39,
Station J,
Toronto, Ont.
M4J 4X8
Order from: University of Toronto Press

Stoddart Publishing Co. Ltd.
34 Lesmill Rd.,
Don Mills, Ont.
M3B 2T6

Talon Books Ltd.
201 - 1019 East Cordova St.,
Vancouver, B.C.
V6A 1M8
Order from: University of Toronto Press

Tundra Books Inc.
1434 St. Catherine St. W.,
Suite 308,
Montreal, Que.
H3G 1R4
Order from: University of Toronto Press

Turnstone Press
607 - 100 Arthur St.,
Winnipeg, Man.
R3B 1H3
Order from: University of Toronto Press

University of Alberta Press
Athabasca Hall,
Rm. 141,
Edmonton, Alta.
T6G 2E8

University of British Columbia Press
6344 Memorial Rd.,
Vancouver, B.C.
V6T 1W5

University of Ottawa Press
603 Cumberland St.,
Ottawa, Ont.
K1N 6N5

University of Toronto Press
10 St. Mary St.,
Suite 700,
Toronto, Ont.
M4V 2W8
Orders:
5201 Dufferin St.,
North York, Ont.
M3H 5T8

Vehicule Press
P.O. Box 125,
Place du Parc Station,
Montreal, Que.
H2W 2M9
Order from: University of Toronto Press

Western Producer Prairie Books
2310 Millar Ave.,
P.O. Box 2500,
Saskatoon, Sask.
S7K 2C4

Wilfrid Laurier University Press
Wilfrid Laurier University,
Waterloo, Ont.
N2L 3C5

The Women's Press
229 College St.,
Suite 204,
Toronto, Ont.
M5T 1R4
Order from: University of Toronto Press

York Press
P.O. Box 1172,
Fredericton, N.B.
E3B 5C8